Easy Casserole Recipes: The Best Casserole Bake Cookbook

OLIVIA NELSON

BREAKFASTS

Eggs Benedict Casserole

Ingredients:

6 English muffins
1 teaspoon onion powder
2 cups 2% milk
1/4 teaspoon paprika
12 ounces Canadian bacon, chopped
salt and pepper to taste
8 eggs

Sauce Ingredients:
1/2 cup butter, melted
4 egg yolks
1 teaspoon Dijon mustard
2 tablespoons lemon juice
1/2 cup heavy whipping cream

Preparation:

Cut the English muffins in half, length-wise then chop into 1-inch chunks.

Broil on an ungreased cookie sheet for 1-2 minutes. Flip bread pieces and broil another 1-2 minutes.

In a greased 9x13 baking dish, arrange half of the Canadian bacon on bottom. Spread the English muffin pieces on top and then the remaining Canadian bacon.

In a bowl, whisk together milk, eggs, onion powder, and salt & pepper to taste. Pour mixture evenly over contents of baking dish. Cover with lid or foil and refrigerate overnight.

30 minutes before baking, remove casserole from refrigerator.

Preheat oven to 375 degrees and sprinkle top of casserole with paprika.

Bake covered for 35 minutes.

Remove cover and bake an additional 10-15 minutes or until center is set.

In a metal bowl (or double boiler) over simmering water, whisk cream, egg yolks, mustard, and lemon juice constantly until it is thick enough to coat the back of a spoon. Reduce heat to low and while whisking constantly, slowly pour in melted butter. Drizzle over top of casserole and serve.

Cinnamon Apple French Toast Casserole

Ingredients:

1 pound sourdough or French bread, cut into chunks
8 large eggs
2 cups milk
2 large apples, chopped
1/2 cup sugar
1/4 cup light brown sugar, unpacked
1/2 cup heavy whipping cream
2 tablespoons vanilla extract
1 1/2 teaspoons ground cinnamon

Topping Ingredients:

1 1/2 teaspoons apple pie spice
1/2 cup salted butter, cut into pieces
3/4 cup all-purpose flour
1 teaspoon cinnamon
3/4 cup brown sugar, packed

Preparation:

Coat a 9x13 baking dish with non-stick cooking spray or grease with butter.

Mix the chopped apples and bread chunks together and spread evenly in the baking dish.

In a bowl, whisk together all other ingredients (except for topping). Pour over top of bread and apple mix. Cover with a lid or foil and refrigerate overnight.

Preheat oven to 350 degrees.

Bake casserole uncovered for approximately 35-40 minutes.

While casserole is in the oven, combine topping ingredients in a bowl. Add the butter and press with fork, mashing together until it has a crumbly consistency.

When casserole is done baking, remove from oven and crumble to topping over the casserole.

Return casserole to the oven and bake for about 5 minutes, until the topping melts.

Serve with warmed syrup.

Sausage & Tater Tot Breakfast Casserole

Ingredients:

1 (30-32 ounce) bag tater tots
2 pounds hot breakfast sausage
2 cups milk
1 1/2 cups cheddar cheese, shredded
1/2 cup mozzarella cheese, shredded
1/4 teaspoon garlic powder
8 eggs
1 teaspoon salt
1/2 teaspoon pepper
1/4 teaspoon onion powder

Preparation:

Preheat oven to 350 degrees.

In a skillet, brown sausage and then drain fat and liquid.

In a bowl, mix tater tots, sausage and cheeses together. Pour into a 9x13 baking dish that has been greased with butter or coated with non-stick spray.

In a bowl, whisk together eggs, milk, garlic powder, onion powder, salt and pepper. Pour mixture on top of ingredients in baking dish.

Bake for 50-60 minutes uncovered or until eggs are firm in center.

Ham and Cheese Hash Brown Casserole

Ingredients:

1 (32 ounce) bag frozen hash browns

1 pound cooked ham, diced

1 1/2 cups parmesan cheese, grated

2 cups sharp cheddar cheese, shredded

1 (16 ounce) container sour cream

2 (10.75 ounce) cans condensed cream of potato soup

Preparation:

Preheat oven to 375 degrees.

Coat a 9x13 inch baking dish with non-stick spray or grease with butter.

In a bowl, combine hash browns, cream of potato soup, ham, cheddar cheese and sour cream. Pour mixture into baking dish. Top with parmesan cheese.

Bake for 60 minutes or until golden brown.

French Toast and Cream Cheese Casserole

Ingredients:

1 (12-14 ounce) loaf sourdough or French bread
3/4 teaspoon ground cinnamon
8 large eggs
2 tablespoons confectioners' sugar
2 1/4 cups whole milk
3 teaspoons vanilla extract, divided
2/3 cup light brown sugar, packed
8 ounces cream cheese, softened to room temperature

Topping Ingredients:

1/3 cup light brown sugar, packed
6 tablespoons unsalted butter, cold and cubed
1/2 teaspoon ground cinnamon
1/3 cup all-purpose flour, leveled
 Garnishes: confectioners' sugar, fresh fruit, and/or maple syrup

Preparation:

Coat a 9x13 baking dish with non-stick spray or grease with butter.

Cube the bread into 1x1-inch pieces. Place half of the cubed bread into the baking dish.

In a bowl, beat the cream cheese with a mixer until smooth. Add in the confectioners' sugar and ¼ teaspoon of vanilla extract and mix.

Spoon cream cheese mix randomly onto bread. Place the rest of the cubed bread on top. Set aside.

In a bowl, whisk together eggs, brown sugar, cinnamon, milk and rest of vanilla until smooth. Pour over top of the bread.

Cover baking dish tightly with plastic wrap and refrigerate for a minimum of 3 hours (or overnight if you can).

Remove pan from refrigerator and preheat oven to 350 degrees.

In a bowl, whisk together flour, brown sugar and cinnamon. With a fork, mash the cubed butter into the mixture until combined. Sprinkle mixture over top of bread.

Bake for 45-55 minutes or until golden brown.

Make Ahead Breakfast Casserole

Ingredients:

3/4 pound uncooked sausage, removed from casings

1/2 cup cheddar cheese, shredded

1/2 cup milk

10 large eggs

2 bell peppers, diced (any color)

1 teaspoon minced garlic

1/2 medium yellow onion, diced

1 cup mushrooms, sliced

4 slices day-old bread

1 cup fresh spinach

salt and fresh ground black pepper

Preparation:

In a skillet, drizzle some olive oil over medium heat. Add in sausage and rosemary, breaking up any large pieces with a spatula. Cook until brown and remove from pan.

Add more olive oil to your skillet, if needed. Add the mushrooms, peppers, onion, garlic, and spinach. Salt and pepper to taste. Stir occasionally until tender, about 6-8 minutes. Set aside.

Coat a 9x13 baking dish generously with non-stick spray or grease with butter.

Break up bread into chunks and spread evenly in the baking dish.

In a bowl, whisk together milk, eggs, and ¼ cup cheese. Pour half of mixture over the top of bread.

Add vegetables and sausage to top of baking dish. Next add the rest of the egg mixture and then ¼ cheese. Season with salt and pepper.

Cover baking dish with foil or plastic wrap and place in refrigerator for at least 2 hours (or overnight, if you can).

Remove casserole from fridge and bring up to room temperature before baking.

Preheat oven to 375 degrees

Bake casserole for about 40-45 minutes or until golden brown.

Italian Breakfast Casserole

Ingredients:

1 (8 ounce) container refrigerated crescent rolls
2 cups frozen diced bell peppers and onions mix
15 slices salami
8 eggs
8 slices ham
1 tablespoon olive oil
1 cup provolone or mozzarella cheese, shredded
salt and pepper to taste

Preparation:

Preheat oven to 350 degrees.

Coat a 9x13 baking dish generously with non-stick spray or grease with butter.

In a skillet, add olive oil over high heat. When oil is hot, add onions and bell peppers. Stir occasionally until softened and blackened around edges. Remove from pan and set aside.

In baking dish, layer crescent rolls, salami and ham.

In a bowl, beat together eggs with salt and pepper. Pour over top of baking dish. Top with onions, peppers and cheese.

Bake for 30 minutes or until golden brown.

Cinnamon Roll Bake

Ingredients:
1 package (0.25 ounces or 2 ¼ teaspoons) active dry yeast (not instant or rapid rise)
1 cup whole milk
1/3 cup unsalted butter, softened
1/2 cup granulated sugar
4 cups all-purpose flour
1 teaspoon salt
2 eggs, room temperature

Filling Ingredients:
1 cup brown sugar, packed
1/3 cup unsalted butter, softened
3 tablespoons cinnamon

Frosting Ingredients:
4 ounces cream cheese, softened
1 teaspoon vanilla
1/4 cup unsalted butter, softened
2 cups powdered sugar

Preparation:

In a saucepan, bring milk to a simmer over medium heat.

Remove from heat, pour into a bowl. Allow to cool for 5 minutes.

When milk has cooled to a warm temperature, mix in the yeast. Let proof for 5 minutes.

In a bowl, mix together eggs, butter, sugar, flour and salt. Mix in the milk and yeast until a dough forms.

On a lightly floured work area, knead the dough for about 5 minutes (or use a dough hook with a stand mixer).

Coat a bowl with non-stick spray. Place the dough in the bowl and turn to coat. Cover with a towel and place in a warm area for 1 hour.

Gently knead the dough to deflate. On a lightly floured surface, shape the dough into a rectangle. Lightly flour a rolling pin and roll it out to a 12x16-inch rectangle.

Mix filling ingredients together in a bowl. Spread mixture evenly over dough but leave a ½-inch border. Roll the dough into a log and pinch the seam closed. Trim the ends off with a knife.

Cut the log into 12 even pieces.

Coat a 9x13 baking dish with non-stick spray or lightly grease with butter.

Space rolls out evenly in dish. Place plastic wrap over baking dish, making sure no dough is exposed and refrigerate overnight.

Remove baking dish from refrigerator. Remove plastic wrap and cover with a towel. Place in a warm area. Let dough rise and come to room temperature for 2 hours prior to baking.

Preheat oven to 350 degrees.

Bake for 35 minutes.

While rolls are baking, prepare the frosting. Mix together cream cheese and butter in a bowl with a hand mixer. Add in the powdered sugar and vanilla and mix until smooth.

While rolls are still hot, add frosting to top.

Veggie Breakfast Casserole

Ingredients:

10 eggs
8 ounces mushrooms, sliced
¼ cup hot sauce (more or less to taste)
⅓ cup milk
2 tablespoons oil
2 bell peppers, diced
2 teaspoons minced garlic
20 ounces hash brown potatoes, thawed
½ red onion, diced
2 cups baby spinach, packed & roughly chopped
1 cup cheddar or Monterey jack cheese, shredded
salt and pepper

Preparation:

Preheat oven to 375 degrees.

Heat 1 tablespoon of oil over medium heat in a skillet. Add in the mushrooms and cook about 4 minutes. Add in garlic, onions and a pinch of salt and cook for 2 minutes. Remove from pan and set aside.

Add 1 tablespoon of oil to pan and cook peppers for 1 minute. Add spinach and cook until it wilts. Remove from heat and set aside.

Coat a 9x13 baking dish with non-stick spray or lightly grease with butter.

Press hash browns into baking dish, making sure they are evenly spread out. Add pepper and mushroom mix to top of potatoes. Set aside.

In a bowl, whisk half and half, eggs, hot sauce and salt & pepper together. Pour over baking dish ingredients. Top with cheese and season with salt and pepper.

Bake uncovered about 45-50 minutes or until golden brown. Cool for 10 minutes before serving.

Biscuit & Egg Casserole

Ingredients:

1 refrigerated container Grand biscuits
8 eggs, beaten
1 cup milk
1 cup mozzarella cheese, shredded
1 cup cheddar cheese, shredded
1 package of Jimmy Dean pre-cooked sausage crumbles
¼ teaspoon salt
⅛ teaspoon black pepper

Preparation:

Preheat oven to 425 degrees.

Coat a 9x13 baking dish with non-stick spray or lightly grease with butter.

Place biscuit dough in bottom of baking dish, pressing firmly into pan. Top with sausage and cheese.

In a bowl, whisk milk, eggs and salt & pepper together until combined. Pour over top of baking dish ingredients.

Bake for 25-30 minutes or until eggs are set. Let cool for 5 minutes before serving.

Blueberry Pancake Casserole

Batter Ingredients:

1 2/3 cups blueberries

1 teaspoon baking soda

2 tablespoons granulated sugar

2 cups buttermilk

zest of 1 small lemon, finely grated

2 eggs

1/2 cup milk

1/2 teaspoon salt

1 teaspoon baking powder

2 1/2 cups all-purpose flour

4 tablespoons unsalted butter, melted

1 1/2 teaspoons pure vanilla extract

Topping Ingredients:

3 tablespoons light brown sugar

1/2 teaspoon cinnamon

1/4 teaspoon salt

4 tablespoons unsalted butter, cold & cut into cubes

1/2 cup all-purpose flour

2 tablespoons granulated sugar

Preparation:

Preheat oven to 350 degrees.

Coat a 9x13 baking dish generously with non-stick spray or grease with butter.

Prepare the topping. In a bowl, mix together both sugars, flour, salt and cinnamon. Add in the butter and work it into the dry ingredients with your fingers until it looks like wet sand. Cover and refrigerate.

Prepare the batter. In a bowl, mix together sugar, flour, baking soda, baking powder and salt.

In a different bowl, whisk together buttermilk, eggs, melted butter, milk, vanilla extract and lemon zest. Add to dry ingredients and use a spatula to combine. Do not overmix (batter will be lumpy).

Pour into baking dish. Top with blueberries.

Remove topping from fridge. Using your fingers, press pieces together to form crumbles and sprinkle on top of ingredients in baking dish.

Bake for 45 minutes or until light golden brown. The edges should begin to pull away from sides of dish. Serve with warm maple syrup.

Biscuits & Gravy with Sausage and Egg Casserole

Ingredients:

1 refrigerated container Grands biscuits
1 (2 3/4 ounce) package peppered gravy mix
1/2 cup milk
6 eggs
1 pound sausage
salt and pepper to taste
1 cup cheese, shredded

Preparation:

Preheat oven to 350 degrees.

Coat a 9x13 baking dish generously with non-stick spray or grease with butter.

In a skillet, brown sausage and then drain.

Cut biscuit dough into 1-inch pieces. Line bottom of baking dish with biscuit pieces.

Top biscuits with sausage and then a layer of cheese.

In a bowl, whisk together, milk, eggs and salt & pepper. Pour over ingredients in baking dish.

Prepare gravy according to directions on package. Pour over top of baking dish.

Bake for 35-45 minutes or until eggs are set.

Apple Fritter Casserole

Ingredients:

5 Granny Smith apples, peeled, cored and diced

6 large croissants, chopped into chunks (baked croissants, not dough)

3 eggs, lightly beaten

1/2 cup heavy cream

2 tablespoons warm water

1/2 cup apple butter (or apple sauce)

1 teaspoon corn starch

6 tablespoons butter

3/4 cup powdered sugar

1/8 teaspoon cinnamon

4 tablespoons heavy cream

1 cup brown sugar, packed

Preparation:

Preheat oven to 375 degrees.

Over medium heat, melt butter in a skillet. Add brown sugar and stir until combined. Add diced apples and stir. Cook until apples are soft, about 5 minutes. Try one to make sure they are desired doneness.

In a bowl, mix together water and cornstarch. Add to apples in skillet and stir. Remove from heat. Set aside.

Coat a 9x13 baking dish generously with non-stick spray or grease with butter.

Place croissant pieces evenly to cover bottom of baking dish. Top with apple mixture and spread evenly with a spatula.

In a bowl, whisk together eggs, apple sauce (or apple butter), heavy cream and cinnamon. Pour over ingredients in baking dish.

Bake for 25 minutes.

While casserole is baking, mix together heavy whipping cream and powdered sugar (1/4 cup at a time) in a bowl. Add a small amount of heavy cream, if needed.

Remove casserole from oven and let cool for 5 minutes. Drizzle icing over casserole and serve.

ENTREES

Hamburger Pie Casserole

Ingredients:

1 pound ground beef
1 (24 ounce) tub refrigerated garlic mashed potatoes (or freshly made)
1 tablespoon Worcestershire sauce
1/2 cup yellow onion, minced
1 cup tomato sauce
1 3/4 pound frozen green beans, thawed
1/2 cup cheddar cheese, shredded
salt & pepper to taste

Preparation:

Preheat oven to 350 degrees.

Coat a 9x13 baking dish generously with non-stick spray or grease with butter.

Over medium heat, cook ground beef and onion in a skillet until browned. Add seasoning, tomato sauce and green beans and mix.

Spread ground beef mixture evenly into bottom of baking dish. Using a spoon, place mounds of mashed potatoes onto ground beef mixture and press to spread slightly. Top with cheese.

Bake for 25-30 minutes or until golden brown.

Chicken Noodle Casserole

Ingredients:

2 cups egg noodles, uncooked

1/2 teaspoon garlic powder

2 cups cooked chicken, shredded

1/2 tablespoon dried minced onion

2 tablespoons butter, melted

1 (10 ounce) package frozen peas and carrots

1 (10 ounce) can cream of chicken soup

1 cup milk

salt and pepper, to taste

1 (10 ounce) can cream of mushroom soup

1/2 teaspoon Italian seasoning

1 (10 ounce) package frozen corn

Preparation:

Preheat oven to 350 degrees.

Coat a 9x13 baking dish generously with non-stick spray or grease with butter.

Cook noodles according to directions on package and drain.

In a bowl, mix all remaining ingredients. Add noodles and stir to combine. Pour into baking dish and cover with foil.

Bake for 30 minutes. Let cool 5 minutes before serving.

Shepherd's Pie Bake

Potato Ingredients:

4 large russet potatoes, peeled and cut into 1 1/2-inch pieces
1/2 cup heavy cream
3/4 teaspoon salt
1/4 cup milk
4 tablespoons butter, cubed
1 cup Swiss cheese, shredded & divided

Beef & Vegetable Ingredients:

2 pounds boneless beef short ribs, trimmed and cut in 1-inch pieces
1 (14.5 ounce) can fire roasted diced tomatoes, undrained
1 large yellow onion, diced
3 stalks celery, diced
3 medium carrots, diced
2 tablespoons low-sodium soy sauce
1/2 teaspoon chili powder
1/4 cup heavy whipping cream
1/2 teaspoon ground black pepper
2 tablespoons all-purpose flour
1 tablespoon ketchup
salt & pepper to taste
1/4 teaspoon dried oregano
1/4 teaspoon paprika

1/4 teaspoon dried parsley
1 1/2 teaspoons salt
3 tablespoons olive oil, divided
Garnish: chopped fresh parsley

Preparation:

Preheat oven to 325 degrees.

Coat a 9x13 baking dish generously with non-stick spray or grease with butter.

Season beef pieces with 1 ½ teaspoons salt and ½ teaspoon pepper.

In a skillet, heat 2 tablespoons of oil over medium high heat. Place beef in pan and brown for 3-5 minutes without touching. Turn pieces and cook an additional 5-7 minutes, stirring occasionally until nicely browned. With a slotted spoon, remove beef and place evenly in bottom of baking dish.

Cover with foil or lid and bake for 30 minutes.

Pour liquid from skillet into a 1-cup measuring cup. Add water to make it a full cup. Set aside.

Over medium high heat, add 1 tablespoon of oil to skillet. Add celery, carrots and onions. Stir frequently and cook for about 5 minutes. Sprinkle with flour and cook while stirring, about 1-2 minutes longer. Flour should be moist. Add in garlic and cook an additional 30 seconds.

Add in ketchup, soy sauce, tomatoes and remaining spices. Bring to a boil. Reduce heat and simmer about 10-15 minutes or until thickened. Mix in ¼ cup heavy cream and set aside.

While vegetables are simmering, boil potatoes with a little salt for 10-15 minutes or until fork tender. Drain and place potatoes in a bowl.

Add milk, heavy cream and butter to hot potatoes and beat until fluffy. Mix in ½ cup cheese and ¾ teaspoon salt. Set aside.

Remove beef from oven. Preheat oven to 425 degrees.

Place vegetable mixture on top of beef in baking dish. Spoon potato mixture on top and spread evenly. Use a fork to create peaks, if desired. Top with ½ cup cheese.

Bake uncovered for 30-35 minutes or until top of potatoes are golden. Let rest for 10 minutes before serving. Garnish with parsley.

Barbecue Pork & Potato Casserole

Ingredients:

4 pounds pre-cooked barbecue pork, frozen or refrigerated

1/2 pound bacon, cooked and chopped

4 tablespoons butter, softened

3 pounds red potatoes

6 green onions, thinly sliced

16 ounces Mexican shredded cheese, divided

8 ounces cream cheese, softened

Preparation:

Heat oven to 400 degrees.

Boil potatoes in salted water until fork tender.

While potatoes are cooking, heat pork according to directions on package.

Coat a 9x13 baking dish generously with non-stick spray or grease with butter.

Drain potatoes and add to a bowl with butter, cream cheese, green onions, bacon and 1/2 of shredded cheese. Mash together until combined.

Spread mashed potatoes into baking dish evenly. Top with

pork and rest of shredded cheese.

Bake in oven for about 5-10 minutes or until cheese is melted and bubbly. Garnish with sliced green onions.

Cheeseburger Slider Casserole

Ingredients:

1 pound ground beef

12 dinner rolls (try to find small brioche rolls if you can)

12 slices sharp cheddar cheese

3 cloves garlic

1 teaspoon kosher salt

1 white onion, chopped

2 teaspoons Worcestershire sauce

1 (10 ounce) can diced tomatoes with green chiles, drained

1 teaspoon black pepper, freshly ground

1 teaspoon mustard powder

1/2 teaspoon paprika

1 teaspoon cumin

Glaze Ingredients:

1 tablespoon mustard

1 tablespoon brown sugar

1 stick unsalted butter

1 tablespoon Worcestershire sauce

sesame seeds

Preparation:

Preheat oven to 350 degrees.

Coat a 9x13 baking dish lightly with non-stick spray or grease with butter.

Add ground beef to a skillet and cook over medium high heat about 3 minutes, untouched. Add garlic, onions, Worcestershire, mustard powder, cumin, paprika and salt & pepper. Stir to combine. Continue cooking until onions are soft and beef is brown.

Drain fat out of pan and add tomatoes, stirring to combine.

Slice rolls in half lengthwise and place bottom halves evenly in baking dish.

Spoon beef mixture onto rolls and top with cheese. Put top halves of buns on cheese.

Prepare the glaze. In a saucepan, melt sugar, butter, mustard and Worcestershire over medium heat until combined. Brush over tops of buns. Garnish with sesame seeds.

Bake for 25-30 minutes or until golden brown.

Baked Ziti Casserole

Ingredients:

1 pound of ground beef
16 ounces dry ziti pasta, cooked according to package directions
2 cups mozzarella cheese, shredded
1 (24 ounce) jar marinara sauce
1 (16 ounce) jar alfredo sauce
½ yellow onion diced
Garnish: grated parmesan cheese

Preparation:

Preheat oven to 350 degrees.

Coat a 9x13 baking dish generously with non-stick spray or grease with butter.

In a skillet, brown ground beef with onion over medium high heat. Drain. Add jar of marinara sauce.

Mix pasta with jar of alfredo sauce. Pour into baking dish evenly.

Add beef and onion mixture to top of pasta. Top with mozzarella cheese.

Cover with foil and bake for 15 minutes. Remove foil and bake an additional 15 minutes. Let rest for 5 minutes before serving.

Salisbury Steak Casserole

Ingredients:

1 1/2 pounds ground beef
1 (24 ounce) tub of pre-made mashed potatoes (or 1 ½ pounds freshly made)
1 (10.5 ounce) can cream of mushroom soup
1 (14.5 ounce) can of French cut green beans, drained
1 (10.5 ounce) can of French onion soup
8 ounces mushrooms, sliced
2 tablespoons Worcestershire sauce
1/4 cup ketchup
1 teaspoon mustard powder
1/8 teaspoon black ground pepper
2 tablespoons all-purpose flour
1/2 cup water
1 packet of dry onion soup mix

Preparation:

Preheat oven to 350 degrees.

Coat a 9x13 baking dish generously with non-stick spray or grease with butter.

Brown ground beef in a skillet. Add 1/3 can French onion soup and pepper.

In a bowl, mix rest of French onion soup, dry onion soup mix, cream of mushroom soup, and flour until smooth. Add Worcestershire sauce, water, ketchup, mustard powder and mushrooms. Stir to combine.

Spread ground beef in bottom of baking dish and then add soup mixture. Top with green beans. Spoon mashed potatoes over green beans and spread with a spatula.

Bake for 20 minutes.

Tamale Pie Bake

Ingredients:

1 pound ground beef
1 box Jiffy corn muffin mix
1 onion, chopped
1 (10 ounce) can red enchilada sauce, divided
1 egg
1/2 cup sour cream
3 cloves garlic, minced
cheddar cheese, shredded
Monterey jack cheese, shredded
1/2 teaspoon salt
1 teaspoon chili powder
1 teaspoon cumin
1/2 cup creamed corn
Small handful cilantro leaves, chopped
Fresh jalapeño, chopped (optional)
Garnish: sour cream

Preparation:

Preheat oven to 400 degrees.

Coat a 9x13 baking dish generously with non-stick spray or grease with butter.

In a bowl, mix together egg, creamed corn, sour cream and Jiffy mix. Spread evenly in baking dish.

Bake for about 15 minutes or until golden brown. Set aside.

While cornbread is baking, brown ground beef and onion in a skillet. Add salt, cumin and chili powder. Stir in garlic and cook an additional 30 seconds. Drain.

Poke holes in cornbread. Pour ½ cup enchilada sauce on top of cornbread. Spread meat mixture onto cornbread. Top with cheese.

Bake for 20 minutes or until golden brown. Drizzle remaining enchilada sauce over top. Garnish with chopped cilantro, diced jalapeño and sour cream

Pizza Pasta Casserole

Ingredients:

16 ounces dry penne pasta, cooked according to package directions

1 pound ground beef

4 ounces pepperoni

1/2 pound pork sausage

2 cups mozzarella cheese, shredded

4 ounces mushrooms, sliced

1 small can olives, sliced

1 (24 ounce) jar pizza or marinara sauce

1 teaspoon oregano

1/2 green bell pepper, chopped

2 cloves garlic, minced

1/2 cup parmesan cheese, grated

1 small yellow or red onion, chopped

Preparation:

Preheat oven to 350 degrees.

Coat a 9x13 baking dish generously with non-stick spray or grease with butter.

In a skillet, brown sausage and ground beef over medium high heat. Drain.

In a bowl, add sausage & beef mixture, bell pepper, onion,

pepperoni, garlic, mushrooms, olives, parmesan and oregano. Stir to combine.

In a separate bowl (or pot that you cooked pasta in), toss pasta with marinara. Pour into baking dish. Add meat & vegetable mixture to top of pasta. Top with 2 cups of mozzarella cheese.

Bake for 25-30 minutes or until golden brown.

Creamy & Cheesy Chicken & Rice Casserole

Ingredients:

2 cups cooked chicken breast, shredded

4 cups cooked brown rice

2 cups cheddar cheese, shredded (plus more for topping)

1 teaspoon black pepper

1/4 cup all-purpose flour

2 cups chicken broth

4 tablespoons butter

2 tablespoons garlic, minced

1 teaspoon kosher salt

Garnishes: shredded cheddar cheese & chopped thyme

Preparation:

Preheat oven to 350 degrees.

Coat a 9x13 baking dish generously with non-stick spray or grease with butter.

In a saucepan, melt butter over medium high heat. Add garlic and cook for 1 minute. Whisk in flour, salt & pepper, and thyme. Slowly whisk in chicken broth. Whisk mixture until it comes to a boil and then stir in cheese until it melts. Mix in chicken and cooked rice.

Pour mixture into baking dish and top with cheese.

Bake for 35-30 minutes or until golden brown.

Macaroni & Cheese Bake

Ingredients:

12 ounces dry macaroni, cooked according to package directions
4 cups sharp cheddar cheese, shredded & divided
1 can condensed cream of cheddar soup
¼ cup flour
1 cup half and half
1½ cups milk
¼ cup butter
½ teaspoon dry mustard powder
½ cup parmesan cheese, grated
salt & pepper to taste
1 teaspoon onion powder

Preparation:

Preheat oven to 425 degrees.

Coat a 9x13 baking dish generously with non-stick spray or grease with butter.

In a saucepan, melt butter over medium heat. Whisk in flour and continue cooking and stirring for 2 minutes. Slowly add milk, cream, onion powder and mustard powder. Whisk to combine. Continue stirring and cooking until thick.

Remove saucepan from heat and add 3 cups of cheddar & ½ cup parmesan cheese. Stir until melted. Add soup and stir to combine.

Pour mixture into baking dish and top with remaining cheddar cheese.

Bake for 20-25 minutes or until golden brown. Let cool for 10 minutes before serving.

Chicken & Rice Enchilada Casserole

Ingredients:

2 cups dry Basmati rice, cooked according to package directions
3 cups cooked chicken, shredded
1 cup white cheddar cheese, shredded
1 cup Monterey Jack cheese, shredded
2 (10 ounce) cans enchilada sauce
1 (16 ounce) can refried beans
1 (11 ounce) can corn, drained
Salt and pepper to taste
Garnish: chopped cilantro

Preparation:

Preheat oven to 350 degrees.

Coat a 9x13 baking dish generously with non-stick spray or grease with butter.

In a bowl, combine refried beans, chicken, enchilada sauce, half of cheddar and half of jack cheese. Season with salt & pepper and add rice. Mix to combine.

Pour mixture into baking dish. Spread corn evenly on top. Add remaining cheese.

Bake for 20-30 minutes or until golden brown. Garnish with cilantro.

Chile Relleno Casserole

Ingredients:

2 (10 ounce) cans whole green chilies

1 1/2 cups sharp cheddar cheese, shredded

8 ounces Monterey jack cheese, cut into strips

8 eggs

2/3 cup milk

1 cup all-purpose flour

1 teaspoon baking powder

Preparation:

Preheat oven to 350 degrees.

Coat a 9x13 baking dish generously with non-stick spray or grease with butter.

Drain green chilies. Insert strips of cheese into chilies. Set chilies in baking dish.

In a bowl, combine milk, eggs, baking powder and flour. Whisk until smooth. Pour over chilies and sprinkle cheese on top.

Bake for 30 minutes.

Meatball Ravioli Casserole

Ingredients:

1 (25 ounce) bag frozen ravioli (or equivalent in refrigerated ravioli)
3 cups mozzarella cheese, shredded
1/3 cup parmesan cheese
1 (14 ounce) bag pre-cooked miniature meatballs, thawed
4 1/2 cups marinara sauce

Preparation:

Preheat oven to 400 degrees.

Coat a 9x13 baking dish generously with non-stick spray or grease with butter.

Pour 1½ cups of marinara in baking dish and spread evenly. Arrange half of ravioli on top of sauce. Add half of the meatballs on top of ravioli.

Pour 1½ cups of marinara on top of baking dish ingredients. Top with half of mozzarella.

Pour 1½ cups of marinara on top of mozzarella. Arrange remaining ravioli on top. Place remaining meatballs on ravioli. Top with parmesan cheese.

Cover with foil and bake for 20 minutes. Remove foil and bake an additional 20-25 minutes. Let cool 10 minutes before serving.

Buffalo Chicken Bake

Ingredients:

2 cups cooked chicken, chopped

1 can refrigerated Grands biscuits

5 tablespoons wing sauce

1 cup alfredo sauce

1/3 cup cooked bacon, chopped

1 cup cheddar cheese, shredded

1 cup mozzarella cheese, shredded

Preparation:

Preheat oven to 375 degrees.

Coat a 9x13 baking dish generously with non-stick spray or grease with butter.

In a large bowl, mix together chicken and buffalo sauce.

Quarter biscuits with a knife. Add biscuits pieces to a bowl with chicken. Mix in bacon, alfredo sauce and half of the cheese. Pour into baking dish and top with other half of cheese.

Bake for 25-30 minutes or until golden brown.

French Onion Chicken Bake

Ingredients:

1 can refrigerated Grands junior biscuits

2 cups cooked chicken, chopped

1/4 cup French fried onions

1 cup cheddar cheese, shredded

1 (10.75 ounce) can cream of chicken soup

8 ounces refrigerated French onion dip

Preparation:

Preheat oven to 350 degrees.

Coat a 9x13 baking dish generously with non-stick spray or grease with butter.

In a bowl, mix together chicken, dip, soup and cheese.

With a knife, cut biscuits into 4 pieces each. Place in bowl with chicken mixture and toss to combine.

Pour into baking dish and top with fried onions.

Bake for 25-30 minutes or until golden brown.

Chicken Alfredo Casserole

Ingredients:

3 boneless, skinless chicken breasts
12 ounces dry penne pasta, cooked according to package directions
¼ teaspoon thyme
2 tablespoons olive oil
4 tablespoons flour
3 cups Italian cheese blend, divided
2 teaspoons minced garlic
3 cups half and half
¼ teaspoon poultry seasoning
3 cups milk
1 stick butter
vegetable oil
1 bottle Italian dressing
salt and pepper to taste
Garnish: Italian seasoning

Preparation:

Slice chicken lengthwise into cutlets. Place chicken into Ziploc bag and pour in Italian dressing. Let marinate overnight or at least 3 hours.

Preheat oven to 350 degrees.

Coat a 9x13 baking dish generously with non-stick spray or grease with butter.

In a small bowl, combine poultry seasoning, thyme and salt & pepper. Season both sides of chicken breast with herb mixture.

In a skillet, heat 2 tablespoons of oil over medium heat. Place chicken in pan. Cook on both sides until chicken is cooked through (about 15-20 minutes). Remove to a plate and set aside.

In a skillet over medium heat, melt butter and then add garlic. Cook for 1-2 minutes. Whisk in flour and stir to combine. Whisk in milk and half & half. Bring to a boil and reduce to a simmer. Continue simmering for about 5 minutes.

Whisk in 1½ cups of cheese. Cook for about 5 minutes or until thick. Remove from heat.

Dice chicken and add to a bowl. Mix in pasta and sauce. Stir to combine.

Pour into baking dish and top with remaining cheese. Season with pepper.

Bake for 30 minutes or until golden brown.

Cornbread Chicken Casserole

Ingredients:

2 cups cooked chicken, chopped
1 box cornbread mix (1 large or 2 small), mixed according to directions on box
1 bag frozen mixed vegetables
1/4 cup diced onions
1/3 cup butter
1 1/4 cup chicken broth
2/3 cup milk
1/3 cup flour
Salt and pepper to taste

Preparation:

Preheat oven to 400 degrees.

Coat a 9x13 baking dish generously with non-stick spray or grease with butter.

Over medium heat, melt butter in a skillet. Add onions and cook for 2 minutes. Add vegetables and cook until heated through.

Add flour and cook about 2 minutes while continuously stirring. Slowly add chicken broth and whisk to combine. Whisk in milk. Continue cooking until thick, about 3 minutes. Add in chicken and cook an additional minute until hot. Remove from heat.

Pour mixture into baking dish. Spread prepared cornbread mix on top and smooth with a spatula.

Bake for 20-25 minutes or until cornbread is done. Let cool for 5 minutes before serving.

Chicken Taquito Casserole

Ingredients:

12 frozen chicken and cheese taquitos
4 ounces sharp cheddar cheese, shredded
8 ounces guacamole
8 ounces salsa
8 ounces sour cream
1 (16 ounce) can refried beans
1 large tomato, chopped
1/2 head iceberg lettuce, chopped

Preparation:

Preheat oven to 400 degrees.

Coat a 9x13 baking dish generously with non-stick spray or grease with butter.

Place frozen taquitos in baking dish and bake for 12 minutes.

Remove baking dish from oven and spread beans evenly over taquitos. Top with ¾ of the cheese and return to oven for 5 minutes.

Remove from oven and garnish with guacamole, lettuce, tomato, salsa, sour cream and remaining cheese.

Italian Sausage & Ravioli Bake

Ingredients:

1 pound mild Italian sausage
1 can fire-roasted tomatoes, undrained
1 large jar of marinara sauce
2 pounds frozen cheese ravioli
2 tablespoons parmesan cheese, grated
2 cups Italian blend cheese, shredded
1/2 cup of water

Preparation:

Preheat oven to 400 degrees.

Coat a 9x13 baking dish generously with non-stick spray or grease with butter.

In a skillet, brown sausage and drain. Mix in pasta sauce, tomatoes and water. Stir to combine.

Pour 1 cup of sausage mixture and spread on bottom of baking dish. Layer half of ravioli on top. Layer one cup of Italian cheese on top.

Pour remaining sausage mixture on top of baking dish ingredients. Layer rest of ravioli on top. Use remaining cup of Italian cheese for the next layer. Top with parmesan cheese.

Cover with foil.

Bake for 30 minutes. Remove foil and bake for an additional 15 minutes or until golden brown.

Chicken & Wild Rice Casserole

Ingredients:

6 ounces dry long grain and wild rice mix, prepared according to package directions
2 cups cooked chicken, chopped
2 tablespoons butter
2 tablespoons fresh basil, chopped
1 (10.5 ounce) can cream of chicken soup
1/3 cup dry white wine or chicken broth
1/3 cup parmesan cheese, grated
1/2 cup sour cream
1 stalk celery, chopped
1 medium onion, chopped

Preparation:

Preheat oven to 350 degrees.

Coat a 9x13 baking dish generously with non-stick spray or grease with butter.

Melt butter in a skillet over medium heat. Add celery and onion and cook until soft. Mix in wine, sour cream, soup and basil. Mix in chicken and cooked rice.

Spread mixture into baking dish evenly. Top with cheese.

Bake for 35 minutes.

Spicy Shrimp and Grits Casserole

Ingredients:

12 ounces pre-cooked large shrimp (16-20 count), peeled & deveined

2 tablespoons butter (plus more for baking dish)

2 cloves garlic, minced

2 cups chicken broth

1 1/4 cups shredded gouda cheese, divided

1 (10 ounce) can diced tomatoes with green chilies, drained

1/2 cup quick-cooking grits (not instant)

2 slices bacon, cooked and chopped

1 jalapeño pepper, seeded & finely chopped

1 bunch scallions, chopped

1/2 red bell pepper, chopped

1 large egg, beaten

salt and freshly ground black pepper, to taste

Preparation:

Preheat oven to 375 degrees.

Coat a 9x13 baking dish generously with non-stick spray or grease with butter.

In a skillet, melt butter over medium high heat. Stir in the bell pepper, jalapeño and green onions. Reduce heat and cook until soft, about 5 minutes.

Mix in chicken broth, diced tomatoes and garlic. Bring to a boil and slowly stir grits into pan. Continue stirring and bring to a boil again. Reduce heat and simmer 5-7 minutes, stirring occasionally. Remove from heat and salt & pepper to taste. Allow to cool for a few minutes.

Add bacon, shrimp, 1 cup of cheese and egg. Spread mixture evenly in baking dish. Top with remaining cheese.

Bake for 30-35 minutes. Let cool 5-10 minutes before serving.

Chili & Cornbread Casserole

Ingredients:

1 (15 ounce) can black beans, rinsed and drained
1 medium yellow onion, chopped
salt and pepper to taste
2 1/2 teaspoons chili powder
1 teaspoon cumin
1 1/2 pounds ground beef
1 (28 ounce) can crushed tomatoes
1 1/2 cups frozen corn
2 cloves of garlic, minced
Garnishes: sour cream and sliced jalapeños

Cornbread Ingredients:

1 cup cornmeal
1 teaspoon salt
2 teaspoons baking powder
1 cup milk
6 tablespoons butter, melted and cooled
2 eggs
1 cup all-purpose flour
1/4 teaspoon baking soda
1 tablespoons sugar

Preparation:

Preheat oven to 375 degrees.

Coat a 9x13 baking dish generously with non-stick spray or grease with butter.

In a skillet, brown ground beef and onion over medium high heat. Mix in chili powder, garlic and cumin. Cook for an additional 30 seconds. Mix in corn and crushed tomatoes. Simmer for 5-7 minutes.

Remove skillet from heat and add in black beans. Stir to combine and salt & pepper to taste.

In a bowl, combine flour, cornmeal, baking powder, baking soda and sugar.

In a different bowl, whisk eggs, butter and milk together. Pour into dry ingredients and stir to combine.

Spread chili on bottom of baking dish. Pour cornbread batter on top.

Bake for 30-35 minutes or until light golden brown.

Chicken Parmesan Casserole

Ingredients:

1 pound cooked chicken, shredded
1 1/2 (32 ounce) jars marinara sauce
1 cup parmesan cheese, shredded
1 cup mozzarella cheese, shredded & divided
2 teaspoons Italian seasoning
16 ounces dry penne pasta, cooked according to package directions
Garnish: chopped basil

Preparation:

Preheat oven to 350 degrees.

Coat a 9x13 baking dish generously with non-stick spray or grease with butter.

In a bowl, mix chicken, pasta, marinara, ½ cup parmesan, ½ cup mozzarella and Italian seasoning. Stir to combine.

Spread mixture into baking dish and cover with foil.

Bake for 30 minutes. Sprinkle remaining cheese on top. Bake an additional 10 minutes.

Million Dollar Spaghetti Bake

Ingredients:

1 pound ground beef
16 ounces dry spaghetti noodles, cooked according to "al dente" package directions
1 (8 ounce) package cream cheese, softened
8 ounces cheddar cheese, shredded
1/2 cup butter, sliced - divided
1/4 cup sour cream
2 cups marinara sauce
1 cup cottage cheese

Preparation:

Preheat oven to 350 degrees.

Coat a 9x13 baking dish generously with non-stick spray or grease with butter.

In a skillet, cook beef over medium high heat until brown. Drain.

In a bowl, mix together cooked beef and marinara.

In a separate bowl, add cottage cheese, sour cream and cream cheese. Stir to combine.

In the bottom of the baking dish, place half of the butter slices evenly. Place half of spaghetti on top. Spread half of cottage cheese mixture oven noodles.

Make another layer with remaining noodles and cottage cheese mixture. Top with remaining butter slices. Pour ground beef mixture over ingredients in baking dish. Cover with foil.

Bake for 30 minutes. Remove foil and cover with cheddar cheese. Bake an additional 15 minutes.

Italian Meatball and Rice Casserole

Ingredients:

26 ounces frozen Italian meatballs

3/4 cups water

2 tablespoons fresh parsley, chopped

1/2 cup mozzarella cheese, shredded

1/4 cup parmesan cheese, grated

3 cups marinara sauce

1 cup dry long grain white rice

1 (14.5 ounce) can diced basil, garlic & oregano tomatoes, undrained

Preparation:

Preheat oven to 375 degrees.

In a bowl, mix together rice, water, tomatoes and marinara. Add meatballs and mix well. Cover with foil.

Bake for 60-75 minutes or until rice is soft. Remove foil and top with parmesan and mozzarella cheese. Return to oven and cook uncovered for an additional 5 minutes.

Swedish Meatball Casserole

Ingredients:

4 ounces mushrooms, sliced
1 (20 ounce) bag frozen pre-cooked meatballs, thawed
2 (1.3-ounce) packages dry brown gravy mix
3 cups dry egg noodles, cooked according to package directions
(subtract 1 minute from shortest cooking time)
2 teaspoons dried parsley flakes
3/4 cup sour cream
2 tablespoons butter
1 teaspoon ground nutmeg
2 cups water
Garnishes: chopped parsley and parmesan cheese

Preparation:

Preheat oven to 350 degrees.

Coat a 9x13 baking dish generously with non-stick spray or grease with butter.

In a skillet, melt butter over medium heat. Add mushrooms and cook about 4 minutes, or until browned.

In a saucepan, mix water and gravy packet together. Bring to a boil and simmer for 3-5 minutes, or until thick. Remove from heat and mix in nutmeg and sour cream.

In a bowl, combine meatballs, mushrooms, noodles, gravy and water mixture and parsley. Toss to coat. Spread mixture into baking dish.

Bake for 30-40 minutes.

Meatball Sub Bake

Ingredients:

1 can refrigerated Grands biscuits
1 bag frozen pre-cooked meatballs
1 1/2 cups mozzarella cheese, shredded
2 cups spaghetti sauce

Preparation:

Preheat oven to 375 degrees.

Coat a 9x13 baking dish generously with non-stick spray or grease with butter.

Cut each biscuit into 8 pieces.

Place the biscuits into the baking dish evenly. Pour sauce onto biscuits. Top with meatballs and sprinkle with cheese.

Bake for 30-40 minutes.

Chicken & Green Chile Enchilada Bake

Ingredients:

1 1/2 cups cooked chicken, shredded
1 (4 ounce) can chopped green chilies
1 (16 ounce) can green enchilada sauce
10 medium tortillas
1 cup sour cream
1 1/2 cups Monterey jack cheese
3 green onions, chopped
3 cilantro springs, chopped
1 medium tomato, chopped

Preparation:

Preheat oven to 425 degrees.

Coat a 9x13 baking dish generously with non-stick spray or grease with butter.

In a bowl, combine chicken with green chilies, half of enchilada sauce and half of cheese.

In a separate bowl, mix sour cream and remaining enchilada sauce. Pour half of sauce into baking dish.

Fill each tortilla with 2-3 tablespoons of chicken mixture, rolling them up and placing them in baking dish. Top with remaining enchilada sauce & sour cream mixture. Cover with the rest of the cheese.

Bake for 25 minutes. Garnish with green onions, tomatoes and cilantro.

Philly Cheesesteak Sandwich Casserole

Ingredients:

1 pound roast beef, thinly sliced
1 sheet sandwich or dinner rolls
8 slices provolone cheese
1 green bell pepper, chopped
1 white onion, chopped
1 cup mushrooms, sliced
1 tablespoon Dijon mustard
2 tablespoons flour
1/2 cup beef stock
2 teaspoons Worcestershire sauce
1/2 cup plus 2 tablespoons butter
salt and pepper, to taste

Preparation:

Preheat oven to 350 degrees.

Coat a 9x13 baking dish generously with non-stick spray or grease with butter.

Slice the sheet of rolls in half, lengthwise so you have 2 large pieces of bread.

In a skillet, cook onions, peppers and mushrooms with 1 tablespoon of butter until soft. Set aside.

Prepare the butter glaze. In a small pan, melt ½ cup of butter with Worcestershire and mustard. Stir to combine and set aside.

In a saucepan, add 2 tablespoons of beet stock, 1 tablespoon of butter and flour. Cook over medium heat until a caramel brown color develops. Add remaining beef stock and bring to a boil. Remove from heat.

Put bottom half of rolls in baking dish. Place roast beef on rolls and then add vegetables. Drizzle some au jus over the veggies and top with cheese. Put top half of rolls on top and then drizzle the butter glaze over them. Cover with foil.

Bake for 25-30 minutes.

Chicken Parmesan Casserole

Ingredients:

1 pound dry penne pasta, cooked according to package directions

2 cups Italian seasoned breadcrumbs

2 cups all-purpose flour

1 pound boneless, skinless chicken breasts

6 cups marinara sauce

1 cup parmesan cheese, grated

2 cups mozzarella cheese, shredded & divided

3 eggs, beaten

1 cup vegetable oil

 Garnish: chopped basil

Preparation:

Preheat oven to 350 degrees.

Coat a 9x13 baking dish generously with non-stick spray or grease with butter.

Slice chicken in half, lengthwise to make thin cutlets. Pound with a meat mallet, if needed to get them about ¼-inch thick.

Heat oil in a skillet over medium heat.

In separate bowls, place breadcrumbs, egg and flour. Coat the chicken first in flour, then egg and then breadcrumbs.

Set breaded chicken gently in pan to brown on each side and cooked through. Remove chicken from pan and let cool for a few minutes before cutting into bite-sized pieces.

In a bowl, mix chicken pieces, pasta, marinara, ½ cup parmesan and 1 cup mozzarella. Stir to combine.

Place mixture in baking dish and cover with foil.

Bake for 30 minutes. Remove from oven and remove foil. Sprinkle the rest of the cheese on top. Bake an additional 10 minutes.

Chicken Spaghetti Casserole

Ingredients:

4 cups cooked chicken, chopped

2 cups sharp cheddar cheese, shredded

1/4 teaspoon ground pepper

1 stick of butter, melted

1 cup Italian breadcrumbs

1/2 teaspoon salt

1/4 cup chicken broth

12 ounces dry spaghetti, cooked according to package directions

16 ounces sour cream

1/2 cup parmesan cheese, grated

1/4 cup dried parsley

1 teaspoon Italian seasoning

1/4 teaspoon cayenne pepper

2 cans cream of chicken soup

Preparation:

Preheat oven to 350 degrees.

Coat a 9x13 baking dish generously with non-stick spray or grease with butter.

In a bowl, mix together all ingredients (except breadcrumbs and cheddar cheese). Pour into baking dish and spread evenly. Top with breadcrumbs and cheddar cheese.

Bake for 50-60 minutes or until golden brown.

Jalapeño Popper Chicken Casserole

Ingredients:

16 ounces dry bowtie pasta, cooked according to package directions
1 1/2 cups cooked chicken, chopped
1/2 cup milk
1 fresh jalapeno, seeded and diced
1 cup water
1 (8 ounce) package cream cheese
1 cup cheddar cheese, shredded
2 cups Monterey jack cheese, shredded
1/2 cup breadcrumbs

Preparation:

Preheat oven to 350 degrees.

Coat a 9x13 baking dish generously with non-stick spray or grease with butter.

In a saucepan, combine water, milk and cream cheese. Add in cheddar and jack cheese. Stir until melted. Add in pasta and most of the diced jalapeños (reserving a few for the top). Add in the chicken and stir to combine.

Spread mixture into baking dish. Top with breadcrumbs and

then jalapeños. Cover with foil.

Bake for 20 minutes. Remove foil and bake an additional 10 minutes.

Chicken Pot Pie Casserole

Ingredients:

1 pound cooked chicken, diced
1/2 teaspoon poultry seasoning
1 cup water
2 cup frozen diced or shredded potatoes, thawed
1 yellow onion, diced
2 cans refrigerated crescent rolls
2 cans cream of chicken soup
12 ounces frozen peas and carrots, thawed
salt and pepper to taste
Olive oil or butter

Preparation:

Preheat oven to 350 degrees.

Coat a 9x13 baking dish generously with non-stick spray or grease with butter.

Unroll 1 can of crescent rolls. Press the perforations in the dough to seal into 1 large sheet. Place dough in baking dish and press into bottom and up sides slightly. Bake for 20 minutes and remove from oven.

In a skillet, cook onions with a little olive oil or butter over medium heat until soft. Add chicken, water, peas & carrots and potatoes. Cook until warmed through. Add poultry seasoning and soup. Continue cooking an additional 5 minutes.

Spread chicken mixture onto baked crust evenly. Unroll other can of crescent rolls and press perforations to seal into 1 large sheet. Place dough on top of chicken mixture and press into sides of baking dish.

Bake for 25 minutes or until golden brown.

Cheesesteak Casserole

Ingredients:

1 1/2 pounds ground beef

16 ounces dry macaroni, cooked according to package directions

2 green bell peppers, chopped

1 teaspoon garlic powder

12 ounces Velveeta

2 yellow onions, chopped

1/2 teaspoon black pepper

1 teaspoon Italian seasoning

Preparation:

Preheat oven to 350 degrees.

Coat a 9x13 baking dish generously with non-stick spray or grease with butter.

In a skillet, brown ground beef with garlic powder, Italian seasoning and pepper. Drain and remove from pan.

In the same skillet, cook onions and peppers until soft. Add beef back to pan and stir to combine. Slice Velveeta and place in pan until melted.

In a large bowl, combine beef mixture and macaroni, mixing

well. Pour in baking dish.

Bake for 15-20 minutes.

Chicken & Biscuits Casserole

Ingredients:

4 cups cooked chicken, chopped

1/2 cup milk

1 medium yellow onion, chopped

1 cup sour cream

1 can cream of chicken soup

1 can refrigerated biscuits

1 1/2 teaspoons butter

1 (4 ounce) jar pimentos, chopped

1 cup mild cheddar cheese, shredded

Preparation:

Preheat oven to 350 degrees.

Coat a 9x13 baking dish generously with non-stick spray or grease with butter.

In a skillet, cook onions with butter until soft. Add in chicken, sour cream, milk, soup and pimentos. Mix well. Pour into baking dish.

Bake for 15 minutes. Remove from oven and Top with cheddar cheese and then biscuits. Bake an additional 20 minutes or until golden brown.

Mexican Tater Tot Casserole

Ingredients:

1 pound ground beef
3 cups Mexican blend cheese, shredded
1 (1 ounce) package taco seasoning mix
1 (4 ounce) can diced green chilies
1 small onion, finely diced
1 clove garlic, minced
1 (10 ounce) can red enchilada sauce
1 (28 ounce) package frozen tater tots
1 (15 ounce) can black beans, rinsed and drained
1 (12 ounce) package frozen corn
Garnishes: olives, cilantro, sour cream, tomatoes

Preparation:

Preheat oven to 375 degrees.

Coat a 9x13 baking dish generously with non-stick spray or grease with butter.

Place tater tots in baking dish and bake for 10 minutes.

Brown the beef and onion in a skillet over medium high heat. Add garlic and cook for an additional minute. Drain. Add in beans, corn, green chilies, taco seasoning mix, and 2 cups of cheese. Mix well.

Remove tater tots from baking dish. Spread beef mixture into dish evenly. Layer tater tots on top of beef. Pour enchilada sauce on top of ingredients in baking dish.

Bake for 30-40 minutes. Top with remaining cheese and bake an additional 5 minutes.

Bacon Cheeseburger Casserole

Ingredients:

1 1/2 pounds ground beef
1 (32 ounce) bag frozen tater tots
16 ounces sour cream
1 (3 ounce) package real bacon bits
1 (10.75 ounce) can cheddar cheese soup
2 cups cheddar cheese, shredded

Preparation:

Preheat oven to 350 degrees.

Coat a 9x13 baking dish generously with non-stick spray or grease with butter.

In a skillet, brown ground beef. Drain.

In a bowl, mix together cooked beef, tater tots, soup, cheddar cheese, bacon and sour cream. Stir to combine. Pour mixture into baking dish.

Bake for 45-50 minutes.

Burrito Casserole

Ingredients:

1 pound ground beef
1/2 cup sour cream
1 small yellow onion, chopped
1 pack large flour tortillas
2 1/2 cups of Mexican blend cheese, shredded
1 can cream of mushroom soup
1 (1.25 ounce) package taco seasoning
1 (16 ounce) can refried beans

Preparation:

Preheat oven to 350 degrees.

Coat a 9x13 baking dish generously with non-stick spray or grease with butter.

In a skillet, brown ground beef and onion. Drain. Add beans and taco seasoning. Cook until heated through. Remove from heat.

In a bowl, mix sour cream with soup. Spread half of mixture evenly in bottom of baking dish.

Layer 3 tortillas on top of soup mixture, overlapping when necessary. Pour half of ground beef mixture onto tortillas and top with 1 cup of cheese. Repeat layers and top with remaining cheese.

Bake for 20 minutes or until golden brown.

Sloppy Joe Bake

Ingredients:

1 pound ground beef
1/2 teaspoons salt
1 can refrigerated Grands Jr. flaky biscuits
2 teaspoons brown sugar
1/2 teaspoons garlic powder
1/2 teaspoon onion powder
2 teaspoons mustard
1 cup cheddar cheese, shredded
1/4 cup water
1 cup ketchup
2 teaspoons Worcestershire sauce

Preparation:

Preheat oven to 350 degrees.

Coat a 9x13 baking dish generously with non-stick spray or grease with butter.

Brown ground beef in a skillet over medium high heat. Drain. Mix in Worcestershire, brown sugar, ketchup, water, onion powder, mustard, garlic powder and salt. Bring to a boil and simmer for 5 minutes. Remove from heat and set aside.

Remove biscuits from can and with a knife, cut each biscuit into

4 pieces. Put pieces into a bowl. Pour in beef mixture and toss to combine. Spread biscuit mixture into baking dish. Sprinkle cheese on top.

Bake for 25-30 minutes.

Taco Casserole

Ingredients:

1 1/4 pounds ground beef
2 cups cooked rice
1 (1.25 ounce) package taco seasoning
1/4 cup water
2 cups Fritos, divided
1 (16 ounce) can refried beans
1 medium yellow onion, chopped
1 (4 ounce) can mild green chilies, diced
2 cups cheddar cheese, shredded
1 cup salsa
salt and pepper to taste

Preparation:

Preheat oven to 350 degrees.

Coat a 9x13 baking dish generously with non-stick spray or grease with butter.

Brown ground beef and onions in a skillet over medium high heat. Season with salt & pepper. Drain. Add taco seasoning mix. Add water, salsa and chilies. Bring to a boil then reduce to a simmer. Simmer covered for 5 minutes.

Remove from heat and mix in beans, rice and cheese. Spread into baking dish evenly. Layer 1 cup of Fritos on top.

Bake for 30-35 minutes. Add remaining Fritos.

Cowboy Lasagna

Ingredients:

12 lasagna noodles, cooked according to package directions
1 pound pre-cooked Italian sausage
1 pound pre-cooked ground beef
12 ounces pepperoni
2 (24 ounce) jars marinara sauce
4 ounces parmesan cheese, grated
4 cups mozzarella cheese, shredded
8 ounces ricotta cheese

Preparation:

Preheat oven to 350 degrees.

Coat a 9x13 baking dish generously with non-stick spray or grease with butter.

In a skillet, brown Italian sausage and ground beef. Drain and remove from heat.

Place a light coating of marinara sauce in bottom of baking dish (about 4-5 tablespoons).

Layer ingredients in this order: 3 lasagna noodles, 1/3 marinara, 1/3 Italian sausage & ground beef mixture, 1/3 pepperoni, 1/3 mozzarella, 1/3 ricotta and 1/3 parmesan. Repeat layers 2 more times.

Bake for 45-55 minutes until golden brown.

Tomato & Beef Noodle Casserole

Ingredients:

1 pound ground beef
12 ounces dry wide egg noodles, cooked according to package directions (subtract 1 minute from shortest cooking time)
1/4 teaspoon pepper
1 can condensed tomato soup
1 cup parmesan cheese, grated
1/4 teaspoon garlic powder
1 cup milk
1 can cream of mushroom soup
salt & pepper to taste
2 tablespoons dried onion flakes
2 teaspoons Worcestershire sauce

Preparation:

Preheat oven to 350 degrees.

Coat a 9x13 baking dish generously with non-stick spray or grease with butter.

In a skillet, brown ground beef over medium high heat. Season with salt. Drain.

In a bowl, mix together both soups, Worcestershire, milk, garlic powder, onion flakes and ¼ teaspoon pepper. Stir to combine.

Add cooked beef and drained noodles. Mix well. Pour into baking dish and top with cheese.

Bake for 25 minutes.

Chicken Fajita Casserole

Ingredients:

4 cups cooked chicken, shredded

2 cups instant rice

1 cup frozen diced onion and bell pepper mix

1 can cream of chicken soup

2 cups Mexican blend cheese, shredded

1 (10-ounce) can Rotel diced tomatoes with chilies, drained

1 (1 ounce) packet fajita seasoning mix

1 1/2 cups chicken broth

1 cup sour cream

Preparation:

Preheat oven to 350 degrees.

Coat a 9x13 baking dish generously with non-stick spray or grease with butter.

In a bowl, mix together uncooked rice, sour cream, drained tomatoes, chicken, chicken broth, onion & bell pepper mix, soup, 1 cup of cheese and the fajita seasoning. Stir to combine. Spread evenly into baking dish. Cover with foil.

Bake for 30 minutes. Remove foil and top with remaining cheese. Cook an additional 5 minutes in oven.

Garlic Parmesan Pasta

Ingredients:

16 ounces dry macaroni (or other small pasta), cooked according to package directions

Topping Ingredients:

2/3 cup Panko breadcrumbs
1 1/2 tablespoons butter

Sauce Ingredients:

1 cup cheddar cheese, shredded
1 cup mozzarella cheese, shredded
1 cup parmesan cheese, grated & divided
1/4 cup butter
salt and pepper to taste
4 cloves garlic, crushed
4 1/2 cups milk, divided
1 tablespoon chicken bouillon powder
1 tablespoon cornstarch
1/4 cup all-purpose flour

Preparation:

Preheat oven to 375 degrees.

Coat a 9x13 baking dish generously with non-stick spray or grease with butter.

Prepare topping. In a skillet, melt butter over medium high heat. Pour in breadcrumbs and stir to coat. Cook until breadcrumbs are golden brown. Remove to a bowl and set aside.

Prepare the sauce. In the same skillet, melt ¼ cup of butter. Add garlic and cook for 1 minute. Whisk in flour and continue whisking for 2 minutes. Reduce heat to low and slowly whisk in 4 cups of milk. Bring to a boil and reduce to a simmer.

In a bowl, whisk together ½ cup milk and cornstarch until smooth. Whisk into skillet ingredients. Cook until thick. Mix in bouillon and season with salt & pepper. Remove from heat and mix in mozzarella, cheddar and ¾ cup parmesan cheese. Stir until melted.

In a large bowl, toss pasta with cheese sauce. Sprinkle breadcrumbs and remainder of parmesan cheese on top.

Bake for 20 minutes or until golden brown. Let cool 5 minutes before serving.

Turkey Noodle Casserole

Ingredients:

12 ounces dry extra-wide egg noodles, cooked according to package directions (subtract 1 minute from shortest cooking time)
3 cups cooked turkey, shredded
1 tablespoon dried thyme
1 cup cooked carrots, diced
1 (12 ounce) jar turkey gravy
1/2 teaspoon salt
1/2 teaspoon pepper

Preparation:

Preheat oven to 350 degrees.

Coat a 9x13 baking dish generously with non-stick spray or grease with butter.

In a large bowl, combine cooked egg noodles, carrots, gravy, turkey, thyme and salt & pepper. Mix well. Pour into baking dish.

Bake for 15 minutes.

Chicken Cordon Bleu Casserole

Casserole Ingredients:

Meat from 1 rotisserie chicken, diced or shredded
1/2 pound deli ham, thinly sliced & chopped
1/2 pound baby Swiss cheese

Sauce Ingredients:

½ teaspoon paprika
4 tablespoons all-purpose flour
¾ teaspoons salt
2 tablespoons fresh lemon juice
4 tablespoons butter
3 cups whole milk
¼ teaspoon pepper
1 tablespoon Dijon mustard

Topping Ingredients:

4 tablespoons butter, melted
1 1/2 cup Panko breadcrumbs
1/2 teaspoons seasoning salt
1 1/2 teaspoons dried parsley

Preparation:

Preheat oven to 350 degrees.

Coat a 9x13 baking dish generously with non-stick spray or grease with butter.

Spread chicken evenly on bottom of baking dish. Layer the ham on the chicken. Top with Swiss cheese.

Prepare the sauce. In a saucepan, melt butter over medium heat. Whisk in flour until smooth. Slowly whisk in milk until combined. Continue cooking, stirring constantly until thick. Mix in mustard, lemon juice, paprika, and salt & pepper. Bring to a boil and remove from heat. Pour evenly over ingredients in baking dish.

Prepare the topping. In a microwaveable bowl, melt butter in microwave. Mix in breadcrumbs and parsley. Sprinkle on top of casserole.

Bake for 45 minutes or until golden brown. Let cool for 5-10 minutes before serving.

Hamburger Mac Casserole

Ingredients:

16 ounces dry macaroni, cooked "al dente" according to package directions
1 1/2 pounds ground beef
1/2 teaspoon oregano
1/2 cup mozzarella cheese, shredded
1/2 cup cheddar cheese, shredded
salt and pepper to taste
1 large onion, diced
1/2 teaspoon paprika
1 (32 ounce) jar marinara sauce
2 cloves garlic, finely chopped
1 tablespoon canola oil

Preparation:

Preheat oven to 400 degrees.

Coat a 9x13 baking dish generously with non-stick spray or grease with butter.

In a skillet, brown the beef and onions in oil. Season with salt & pepper. Add in the paprika, oregano and garlic. Pour in marinara and bring to a boil. Reduce to a simmer and cook for 15 minutes, stirring occasionally.

Add cooked macaroni to skillet and mix well. Pour mixture into baking dish and spread evenly. Top with cheese.

Bake for 15-20 minutes or until golden brown.

Stuffed Pepper Casserole

Ingredients:

1 1/2 pounds pre-cooked ground beef or turkey, drained
2 cups marinara sauce
8 green onions, chopped
5 bell peppers, any color
2 teaspoons cumin
1 medium Vidalia onion, chopped
8 ounces white mushrooms, sliced
1 teaspoon pepper
2 1/2 cups Mexican blend cheese, shredded
1 cup dry instant white rice
1 teaspoon kosher salt
Garnish: chopped cilantro

Preparation:

Preheat oven to 375 degrees.

Coat a 9x13 baking dish generously with non-stick spray or grease with butter.

In a bowl, mix together everything except for ½ cup of cheese. Pour into baking dish and top with the reserved ½ cup of cheese. Cover with foil.

Bake for 45-50 minutes. Remove foil and bake for 10 minutes

or until golden brown.

Million Dollar Casserole

Ingredients:

16 ounces dry spaghetti, cooked "al dente" according to package directions
1 1/2 pounds ground beef
1/2 pound bacon, cooked and chopped
1 1/2 cups marinara sauce
1 red bell pepper, chopped
1/2 cup cheddar cheese, shredded
1 yellow onion, chopped
8 ounces cream cheese, softened
8 ounces cottage cheese
2 teaspoons garlic, crushed
2 tablespoons vegetable oil
salt and pepper to taste
1/4 cup sour cream

Preparation:

Preheat oven to 350 degrees.

Coat a 9x13 baking dish generously with non-stick spray or grease with butter.

In a skillet, cook onion and bell pepper in oil until soft. Add garlic and cook for 1 more minute. Turn off heat and add cooked bacon. Stir to combine. Remove from pan and set aside.

In the now empty skillet, brown ground beef. Season with salt & pepper. Return onion & bacon mixture to skillet. Pour in marinara and cook until heated through.

In a bowl, combine sour cream, cream cheese and cottage cheese. Mix well.

Spread half of cooked noodles in bottom of baking dish. Top with cheese mixture. Next spread remaining noodles and top with beef mixture.

Bake for 25 minutes. Remove from oven and top with cheddar cheese. Bake an additional 10-15 minutes.

Farmer's Casserole

Ingredients:

4 eggs, beaten
1 cup ham, cubed
3 cups frozen hash browns
1/4 cup green onion, finely chopped
1 (12 ounce) can evaporated milk
3/4 cup Monterey jack cheese, shredded
1/4 teaspoon black pepper
1/2 teaspoon salt

Preparation:

Coat a 9x13 baking dish generously with non-stick spray or grease with butter.

In a bowl, whisk together eggs, milk and seasonings. Set aside.

Spread potatoes on bottom of baking dish evenly. Top with onions, ham and cheese. Pour milk mixture over top of ingredients in baking dish. Cover with foil and refrigerate overnight.

Remove casserole 30 minutes prior to baking.

Preheat oven to 350 degrees.

Bake for 40-50 minutes or until set. Let stand 5 minutes.

French Onion Chicken & Noodle Casserole

Ingredients:

4 cups cooked chicken, chopped
1 (16 ounce) container French onion dip
12 ounces dry egg noodles, cooked according to package directions (subtract 1 minute from shortest cooking time)
1 cup French fried onions, crushed
2 cans cream of chicken soup
1 cup cheddar cheese, shredded

Preparation:

Preheat oven to 350 degrees.

Coat a 9x13 baking dish generously with non-stick spray or grease with butter.

In a bowl, mix together soup, chicken, cheese and dip. Add cooked noodles and toss to coat. Pour into baking dish and top with fried onions.

Bake for 25-30 minutes.

Chicken Caesar & Bacon Casserole

Ingredients:

1 can refrigerated buttermilk biscuits
3/4 cup bacon, cooked & chopped
2 cups cooked chicken, chopped
1/4 cup water
1/4 teaspoon pepper
2 cups Italian blend cheese, shredded
8 ounces garlic & herb spreadable cheese (such as Laughing Cow)
2 cups fresh spinach, chopped
1/2 cup Caesar dressing

Preparation:

Preheat oven to 350 degrees.

Coat a 9x13 baking dish generously with non-stick spray or grease with butter.

In a bowl, whisk together dressing, water, spreadable cheese and pepper.

Remove biscuits from can. Cut each biscuit into 6 pieces. Add to bowl with dressing mixture and toss to coat. Add in spinach, chicken, half of the bacon and half of Italian blend cheese. Mix well. Pour mixture into baking dish. Sprinkle other half of Italian cheese and remaining bacon on top.

Bake 35-40 minutes or until golden brown.

Chicken Tater Tot Bake

Ingredients:

1 (2 pound) bag frozen tater tots
3 cups cooked chicken, chopped
1 (1 ounce) package ranch dressing mix
1 can cream of chicken soup
16 ounces sour cream
1 (3 ounce) bag real bacon pieces
2 cups cheddar cheese, shredded

Preparation:

Preheat oven to 350 degrees.

Coat a 9x13 baking dish generously with non-stick spray or grease with butter.

In a bowl, combine soup, bacon, sour cream, ranch dressing mix, chicken and cheese. Add tater tots and toss to coat. Spread mixture evenly into baking dish.

Bake for 40-45 minutes.

Chili Spaghetti Bake

Ingredients:

16 ounces dry spaghetti, cooked "al dente" according to package directions

1 1/2 pounds ground beef

1 (14.5 ounce) can diced tomatoes

2 tablespoons dried minced onion flakes

1 (2.8oz) can French fried onions

1 (15 ounce) can chili without beans

1 1/2 cups cheddar cheese, shredded

1/4 teaspoon garlic powder

8 ounces sour cream

2 teaspoons chili powder

Preparation:

Preheat oven to 350 degrees.

Coat a 9x13 baking dish generously with non-stick spray or grease with butter.

In a skillet, brown ground beef over medium high heat. Season with salt & pepper. Drain.

In a bowl, mix together cooked ground beef, undrained tomatoes, chili powder, onion flakes, garlic powder, sour cream, cooked noodles and the can of chili. Pour into baking dish and spread evenly. Sprinkle cheese and fried onions on top.

Bake for 30 minutes or until golden brown.

Chicken Lasagna Bake

Ingredients:

15 no-boil lasagna noodles
3 cups cooked chicken, shredded
1 cup water
1/4 cup seasoned breadcrumbs
12 ounces frozen peas
1/2 cup Swiss cheese
1/2 cup parmesan cheese
Garnish: chopped flat leaf parsley

Sauce Ingredients:

5 cups milk
3/4 teaspoon salt
6 tablespoons all-purpose flour
1/2 teaspoon poultry seasoning
6 tablespoons butter
1 1/2 tablespoons garlic, minced

Preparation:

Preheat oven to 400 degrees.

Prepare the sauce. In a saucepan, melt butter over medium high heat. Add garlic and cook for 1 minute. Whisk in flour, salt and poultry seasoning. Cook an additional 1-2 minutes. Slowly whisk in milk. Reduce heat and cook until thick. Remove from heat and set aside.

Layer the lasagna. Place 5 broken lasagna noodles in the bottom of baking dish. Then add 1½ cups of sauce, 1/3 cup of water, half of the peas, half of the chicken and ¼ cup parmesan cheese. Repeat the layering steps once.

Top ingredients in baking dish with broken 5 lasagna noodles, 1½ cups of sauce, 1/3 cup of water and ½ cup of Swiss cheese. Cover with foil.

Bake for 40 minutes. Remove foil and top with breadcrumbs. Bake 5-10 minutes until golden brown. Let cool 10 minutes before serving.

Smoked Sausage Alfredo Casserole

Ingredients:

12 ounce fully-cooked smoked sausage, sliced into ¼-inch pieces

16 ounces dry penne pasta, cooked according to package directions

2 cups mozzarella cheese, shredded & divided

1/2 cup parmesan cheese, grated

3 tablespoons butter

2 tablespoons fresh parsley, chopped

1/4 teaspoon red pepper flakes

2 cups half and half

3 tablespoons all-purpose flour

1/4 teaspoon cayenne pepper

2 cloves garlic, minced

1 cup chicken broth

1/2 teaspoon salt

1/4 teaspoon pepper

Preparation:

Preheat oven to broil.

In a skillet, melt butter over medium heat. Add garlic and cook an additional minute. Whisk in flour. When flour has absorbed butter, slowly whisk in chicken broth. Mix in half & half, cayenne, red pepper flakes and salt & pepper. Reduce to a simmer and cook for 5 minutes.

Add mozzarella and parmesan to skillet. Stir until melted. Add sausage and parsley. Salt & pepper to taste. Spread mixture evenly into baking dish. Top with remaining mozzarella.

Broil for 2-3 minutes or until golden brown.

Reuben Casserole

Ingredients:

1 pound pastrami or corned beef, thinly sliced
2 teaspoons caraway seeds
1 (14.5 ounce) can sauerkraut
4 cups Swiss Cheese, shredded
1/4 cup mustard
6 slices dark rye bread
1 cup dill pickles, chopped
1/3 cup Thousand Island dressing
3 large eggs
1 cup milk

Preparation:

Preheat oven to 350 degrees.

Coat a 9x13 baking dish generously with non-stick spray or grease with butter.

Cut 4 pieces of bread into cubes. In a food processor, pulse remaining bread slices into fine breadcrumbs. Set aside.

Place bread cubes evenly into baking dish. Top with half of the pastrami. Then layer with sauerkraut, pickles, 2 cups of cheese and half of the caraway seeds. Top with remaining pastrami, caraway seeds and cheese.

In a bowl, combine salad dressing, mustard and milk with a whisk. Whisk in eggs until combined. Pour over ingredients in baking dish and sprinkle with breadcrumbs.

Bake for 40-45 minutes or until golden brown.

Taco Macaroni Casserole

Ingredients:

2 pounds ground beef
16 ounces dry macaroni, cooked "al dente" according to
package directions
1 tablespoons garlic, minced
1 cup sour cream
2 tablespoons onions, minced
3/4 cup water
2 packages taco seasoning mix
salt and pepper to taste
2 cups sharp cheddar cheese, shredded
2 cups salsa
8 ounces cream cheese

Preparation:

Preheat oven to 350 degrees.

Brown ground beef and onions in a skillet over medium high
heat. Add garlic and cook 1 minute. Mix in taco seasoning and
salsa. Reduce heat to medium and simmer for 5 minutes.

Add cook noodles, sour cream, cream cheese and water to
skillet. Mix until well combined. Pour evenly into baking dish
and top with cheddar cheese. Season with salt & pepper.

Bake for 20-25 minutes or until golden brown.

Cabbage Roll Casserole

Ingredients:

1 pound ground pork or beef
2 cups cooked white or brown rice
1 cup tomato sauce
1 (28 ounce) can diced tomatoes
1 large head of cabbage, coarsely chopped
3 cloves garlic, crushed
1 teaspoon thyme
1 tablespoon tomato paste
1 tablespoon olive oil
1 large yellow onion, diced
1/2 teaspoon pepper
1 teaspoon paprika
2 cups Gruyere or Monterey jack cheese, shredded
1 egg
1/4 cup milk

Preparation:

Preheat oven to 375 degrees.

Coat a 9x13 baking dish generously with non-stick spray or grease with butter.

In a skillet, brown ground beef and onion. Add garlic and cook 1 minute. Drain. Add in undrained tomatoes, tomato sauce, tomato paste, paprika and thyme. Salt & pepper to taste. Bring to a boil and reduce to a simmer for 10 minutes until thick. Remove from heat. Add cooked rice and mix well to combine. Set aside.

In a skillet, heat 1 tablespoon of oil and half of chopped cabbage. Cook about 5 minutes or until soft. Remove cabbage from pan and spread evenly in baking dish. Add remaining chopped cabbage to skillet and cook until soft. Set aside.

Top cabbage in baking dish with half of meat mixture. Spread remaining cabbage from skillet on top. Top with rest of meat mixture. Cover with foil.

Bake for 45 minutes

In a bowl, whisk together egg and milk. Stir in cheese. Remove foil from casserole and pour mixture on top. Bake uncovered for 20 minutes.

Loaded Baked Potato & Chicken Casserole

Ingredients:

4 medium-sized potatoes (about 1.5 pounds), peeled and cut into pieces
1 pound cooked chicken, cubed
1 1/2 cups sharp cheddar cheese, shredded
4 slices bacon, cooked & chopped
4 green onions, sliced
1/2 teaspoon ground black pepper
1/2 teaspoon salt
1/2 teaspoon paprika
1/2 cup heavy cream

Preparation:

Preheat oven to 350 degrees.

Coat a 9x13 baking dish generously with non-stick spray or grease with butter.

Place half of potatoes in baking dish and spread evenly. Top with chicken. Season with ¼ teaspoon each of paprika, salt & pepper. Add half the bacon, ½ cup of cheese and half of the green onions.

Place remaining potatoes on top of ingredients in baking dish. Layer with rest of bacon, ½ cup of cheese and ¼ teaspoon each of paprika, salt & pepper. Pour heavy cream on top evenly. Cover with foil.

Bake for 1 hour. Remove foil and bake for an additional 30 minutes. When 10 minutes of cooking time is left, top with remaining cheese and green onions.

Spinach & Cheese Tortellini Bake

Ingredients:

12 ounces cheese tortellini, cooked according to package directions

4 strips bacon, cooked and chopped, reserve fat from pan

2 cups fresh spinach, chopped

2 tablespoons all-purpose flour

2 teaspoons lemon juice

1 teaspoon dried basil

1/8 teaspoon black pepper

3/4 teaspoon salt

3 teaspoons minced garlic

2 cups milk

3/4 cup mozzarella cheese, shredded

3/4 cup parmesan cheese, grated

Preparation:

Preheat oven to 350 degrees.

Coat a 9x13 baking dish generously with non-stick spray or grease with butter.

In a skillet, add reserved bacon fat and cook garlic for 1 minute. Whisk in flour until fat is absorbed. Slowly whisk in milk until smooth. Add lemon juice, basil, and salt & pepper. Bring to a boil and reduce to a simmer.

In a large pot, add hot tortellini, bacon, spinach and most of mozzarella and parmesan cheese. Cook over low heat and add sauce. Stir to combine. Pour into baking dish and spread evenly. Top with remaining cheese. Cover with foil.

Bake for 20 minutes. Remove foil and bake for 5 more minutes.

Teriyaki Chicken Casserole

Ingredients:

1 small bag fresh stir fry vegetables (broccoli, sprouts, carrots and snow peas), steamed
1 breast of chicken
3 cups pre-made fried rice

Sauce Ingredients:

3/4 cup low sodium soy sauce
1/3 cup brown sugar
1/2 cup water
1 teaspoon sesame oil
2 tablespoons cold water
1 small garlic clove, finely minced
2 tablespoons cornstarch
3/4 teaspoon ground ginger
1 tablespoon honey

Preparation:

Preheat oven to 350 degrees.

Coat a 9x13 baking dish generously with non-stick spray or grease with butter.

Prepare teriyaki sauce. In a saucepan, combine water, brown sugar, soy sauce, honey, sesame oil, garlic and ground ginger. Bring to a boil for 1 minute and reduce to a simmer.

In a bowl, combine cornstarch with water. Add 1 teaspoon of prepared sauce and mix. Slowly whisk contents of bowl into simmering sauce. Simmer until thickened. Remove from heat and set aside.

Set chicken in baking dish with 1 cup of teriyaki sauce poured over top.

Bake for 30 minutes. Remove from oven and shred chicken with forks.

In a bowl, combine shredded chicken, rice, steamed vegetables and 3 tablespoons of teriyaki sauce. Spread evenly into baking dish.

Bake for 15 minutes. Drizzle with teriyaki sauce and serve.

Tuna Noodle Casserole

Ingredients:

2 cans tuna, drained
8 ounces dry spiral pasta, cooked "al dente" according to package directions
1 can cream of mushroom soup
1/2 large white onion, diced
1 teaspoon garlic powder
1/2 cup sour cream
4 ounces cream cheese
3/4 cup milk
1 cup French fried onions
1 cup Colby jack cheese, shredded
4 mini bella mushrooms, sliced
3 tablespoons extra virgin olive oil
salt and pepper to taste

Preparation:

Preheat oven to 375 degrees.

Coat a 9x13 baking dish generously with non-stick spray or grease with butter.

In a skillet, heat olive oil over medium heat. Add mushrooms and onions. Cook until soft. Add in milk, cream cheese, soup, sour cream and garlic powder. Stir until heated through. Season to taste with salt & pepper. Add cooked pasta to pan and mix well. Pour into baking dish and top with shredded cheese. Top with fried onions.

Bake for 10 minutes or until onions are golden brown.

Chicken Marsala Casserole

Ingredients:

2 cups cooked chicken, chopped

1 cup dry brown rice

1 1/2 tablespoons all-purpose flour

1/4 teaspoon black pepper

1/2 cup marsala or white wine

16 ounces mushrooms, sliced

2 cups low-sodium chicken broth

5 cloves garlic, minced

1 teaspoon salt

1/2 cup half & half

2 tablespoons olive oil

1 small yellow onion, diced

1/4 cup fresh parsley, chopped

2 tablespoons parmesan cheese, grated

Preparation:

Preheat oven to 375 degrees.

Coat a 9x13 baking dish generously with non-stick spray or grease with butter.

In a skillet, add butter and oil over medium high heat until melted. Add mushrooms and onions and cook until soft. Add garlic and cook for 1 minute. Salt & pepper to taste. Add flour and stir until liquid is absorbed. Add cream and wine. Bring to a boil and reduce to a simmer until thick, about 3 minutes. Mix in chicken broth.

Spread rice evenly in baking dish. Layer the chicken on the rice and then pour mushroom sauce over the top. Sprinkle parsley on top of casserole. Cover with foil.

Bake for 45 minutes if using brown rice, 35 minutes for white rice. Remove foil and top with parmesan cheese. Bake an additional 5 minutes.

Chicken & Green Bean Casserole

Ingredients:

6 boneless skinless chicken breasts
1 (6 ounce) package chicken stuffing mix, prepared according to package directions
1/2 pound fresh green beans, trimmed, cut into 1-inch pieces
5 ounces cream cheese
1 tablespoon butter
1 3/4 cups chicken broth
1/2 teaspoon black pepper
1/4 cup all-purpose flour

Preparation:

Preheat oven to 400 degrees.

Coat a 9x13 baking dish generously with non-stick spray or grease with butter.

In a skillet over medium heat, melt butter. Add chicken and season with salt & pepper. Cook about 5 minutes on each side until fully cooked. Remove chicken from pan and place in baking dish.

In the same skillet, add green beans. Cook for about 6 minutes or until crisp-tender. Stir in flour and cook for 1 minute. Pour in broth and simmer for 3 minutes while stirring. Stir in cream cheese until melted. Pour over top of chicken in baking dish. Top with prepared stuffing.

Bake for 30 minutes.

Chicken Cordon Bleu Lasagna

Ingredients:

9 lasagna noodles, cooked according to package directions
3 cups Swiss cheese, shredded
2 cups bacon, cooked & chopped
1½ cups cooked ham, diced
4 1/2 cups cooked chicken, chopped

Sauce Ingredients:

1/2 cup all-purpose flour
1 teaspoon garlic salt
1 teaspoon garlic powder
1/2 teaspoon salt
16 ounces cream cheese, softened
1/2 cup butter
4 cups milk
1/4 teaspoon white pepper

Preparation:

Preheat oven to 350 degrees.

Coat a 9x13 baking dish generously with non-stick spray or grease with butter.

In a saucepan, melt butter over medium heat. Add flour and stir until butter is absorbed. Slowly whisk in milk. Add in garlic salt, garlic powder and salt & pepper. Whisk ingredients together and bring to a boil. Stir in cream cheese until melted. Remove from heat and set aside.

Lay 3 lasagna noodles in baking dish. Add 1/3 of the chicken and then 1/3 of the ham. Next add 1/3 of the sauce and then 1/3 of the cheese. Top with 1/3 of the bacon. Repeat these steps 2 more times.

Bake for 50-60 minutes.

Chicken Enchilada Casserole

Ingredients:

1 pound cooked chicken, shredded

8 small flour tortillas

2 1/2 cups enchilada sauce

1 (16 ounce) can refried beans

3 cups Monterey jack cheese, shredded

Garnishes: chopped cilantro and sliced green onions

Preparation:

Preheat oven to 375 degrees.

Coat a 9x13 baking dish generously with non-stick spray or grease with butter. Place about 4 tablespoons of enchilada sauce in bottom of dish and spread.

Put 4 tortillas in baking dish, overlapped to cover bottom. Next layer on top, half of beans, half of chicken, 1 cup of cheese and 1 cup of enchilada sauce. Repeat steps 1 more time, starting with tortillas. Top with remaining enchilada sauce and cheese. Cover with foil.

Bake for 30 minutes. Remove foil and bake for 5 more minutes. Let cool for 15 minutes before serving.

Amish Country Casserole

Ingredients:

12 ounces medium egg noodles, cooked according to package directions (subtract 1 minute from shortest cooking time)
1 pound ground beef
1 cup milk
1/8 teaspoon salt
2 tablespoons onion flakes
1/4 teaspoon pepper
1/4 cup parmesan cheese, grated
2 teaspoons Worcestershire Sauce
1 (10.75 ounce) can cream of mushroom soup
1 (10.75 ounce) can tomato soup
1/4 teaspoon garlic

Preparation:

Preheat oven to 350 degrees.

Coat a 9x13 baking dish generously with non-stick spray or grease with butter.

In a skillet, brown ground beef over medium high heat. Drain.

In a bowl, mix together milk, both soups, Worcestershire, onion flakes, garlic and salt & pepper. Add cooked beef and noodles. Mix to combine. Pour into baking dish and top with cheese.

Bake 30 minutes.

Mexican Lasagna

Ingredients:

1 1/4 pounds ground beef or ground turkey
1 teaspoon salt
3 cloves garlic, minced
1 red bell pepper, chopped
2 medium onions, chopped
1/2 teaspoon dried oregano
2 cups mild cheddar cheese, shredded
1 (7 ounce) can diced green chilies
1 tablespoon ground coriander seeds
1 (16 ounce) can refried beans
1 (28 ounce) can fire-roasted diced tomatoes
12 yellow corn tortillas
1/4 teaspoon cayenne
2 cups Monterey jack cheese, shredded
1 tablespoon ground cumin
1 tablespoon chili powder
olive oil
Garnishes: sour cream, avocado, cilantro, iceberg lettuce

Preparation:

Preheat oven to 350 degrees.

Coat a 9x13 baking dish generously with non-stick spray or grease with butter.

In a skillet, brown ground beef over medium high heat in some olive oil. Salt & pepper to taste. Add coriander, cayenne, chili powder and cumin. Remove with a slotted spoon into a bowl and set aside.

Prepare the sauce. In the same skillet, add some olive oil with bell peppers and onions. Cook until soft. Add garlic and cook for 1 minute. Add in green chilies, tomatoes and oregano. Bring to a boil and reduce to a simmer for about 15 minutes.

Make a single layer of 4 tortillas in bottom of baking dish, overlapping where necessary. Then add half of beans and spread over tortillas. Add half of beef, 1/3 of cheese and half of the sauce. Repeat these layers once.

Top ingredients in baking dish with remaining tortillas and top with rest of cheese.

Bake for 35 minutes. Let cool for 15 minutes before serving.

Spinach & Artichoke Ravioli Casserole

Ingredients:

25 ounces frozen ravioli

5 ounces fresh spinach, chopped

1 cup Italian blend cheese, shredded

2 cups alfredo sauce

1 (16 ounce) can artichoke hearts, diced

1/4 cup chicken broth

2 tablespoons pesto

Preparation:

Preheat oven to 375 degrees.

Coat a 9x13 baking dish generously with non-stick spray or grease with butter.

In a bowl, mix together pesto, artichoke and spinach until combined.

In a different bowl, mix together broth and alfredo sauce. Spread 1/3 of mixture on bottom of baking dish.

Place half of spinach mixture in baking dish on sauce. Layer half over ravioli evenly on spinach.

Repeat layers with 1/3 of sauce, half of spinach and then half of ravioli. Top with remaining 1/3 of sauce.

Bake for 30 minutes. Top with cheese and broil for 3-5 minutes until golden brown.

Sloppy Joe Tater Tot Casserole

Ingredients:

1 1/4 pounds ground beef
1 medium yellow onion, chopped
1/4 cup brown sugar
3/4 teaspoon vinegar
2 teaspoons steak seasoning
1 tablespoon oil
1 tablespoon Worcestershire sauce
2 cups tomato sauce
1 bag frozen tater tots
2 tablespoons tomato paste
1 cup sharp cheddar cheese, shredded
salt and pepper to taste

Preparation:

Preheat oven to 350 degrees.

Coat a 9x13 baking dish generously with non-stick spray or grease with butter.

In a skillet brown ground beef and onion in oil over medium heat. Add steak seasoning, brown sugar and Worcestershire. Mix well. Add vinegar, tomato paste and tomato sauce. Bring to simmer for about 5 minutes.

Spread half of tater tots in baking dish. Pour beef and tomato mixture on top. Top with other half of tater tots. Season with salt & pepper. Top with cheese.

Bake for 40-45 minutes. Let cool for 10 minutes before serving.

Chicken Caprese & Quinoa Casserole

Ingredients:

3 cups cooked chicken, diced
1 cup dry quinoa
1 cup mozzarella cheese, shredded & divided
salt and pepper to taste
1 tablespoon balsamic vinegar
2 tablespoons tomato paste
1/4 cup parmesan cheese, grated
1/4 teaspoon crushed red pepper
1 cup grape tomatoes, halved
2 cups chicken broth
1/4 cup half and half
1 (12 ounce) can crushed tomatoes
1/2 cup fresh basil, chopped

Preparation:

Preheat oven to 375 degrees.

Coat a 9x13 baking dish generously with non-stick spray or grease with butter.

Prepare quinoa. Rinse quinoa and soak in warm water for 10 minutes. In a saucepan, boil chicken broth and add drained quinoa. Reduce heat to a simmer, cover and cook for 12-15 minutes. Remove from heat and let quinoa sit covered for 5 minutes. Fluff with fork and set aside.

Prepare sauce. In a saucepan, combine vinegar, tomato paste and crushed tomatoes and bring to a simmer over medium heat. Add in half & half, red pepper flakes and salt & pepper. Cook until heated through. Remove from heat.

In a bowl, combine quinoa, chicken, parmesan and ½ cup of mozzarella. Stir in sauce and mix well.

Spread mixture evenly into baking dish and top with rest of mozzarella and grape tomatoes.

Bake for 15 minutes,

Beef Stroganoff Casserole

Ingredients:

12 ounces dry extra-wide egg noodles, cooked according to package directions (subtract 1 minute from shortest cooking time)
1 pound ground beef
1 can cream of mushroom soup
3 tablespoons flour
1 1/2 cups beef broth
1 cup sour cream
1/2 yellow onion, chopped
2 cloves garlic, minced
3 tablespoons butter
1 cup parmesan cheese
salt & pepper to taste

Preparation:

Preheat oven to 350 degrees.

Coat a 9x13 baking dish generously with non-stick spray or grease with butter.

In a skillet, brown ground beef and onion. Add garlic and cook 1 minute. Drain. Remove from pan.

In the same skillet, add butter over medium heat until melted. Whisk in flour until butter is absorbed. Slowly whisk in broth until smooth. Bring to a boil and reduce to a simmer for 2-3 minutes. Whisk in soup, sour cream and salt & pepper to taste.

In a large bowl, toss cooked noodles with beef and sauce mixture until coated. Pour into baking dish and top with cheese.

Bake for 20 minutes.

Mexican Cornbread Casserole

Ingredients:

1 pound ground beef
1 (14 ounce) can cream-style corn
1 (14 ounce) can corn kernels, drained
1 (4-ounce) can diced green chilies, drained
1 1/2 cups cheddar cheese, shredded
1 package taco seasoning mix
2 (8.5 ounce) boxes corn muffin mix, prepared according to package directions

Preparation:

Preheat oven to 350 degrees.

Coat a 9x13 baking dish generously with non-stick spray or grease with butter.

Brown the ground beef in a skillet over medium high heat. Add taco seasoning mix according to the direction on package.

In the bowl with the prepared corn muffin mix, add half of corn kernels and half of cream corn. Stir to combine. Pour half of batter into baking dish. Add ground beef on top. Add rest of corn kernels and then rest of cream corn, spreading evenly. Top with half of cheese and green chilies. Spread the rest of muffin batter on top and add remaining cheese.

Bake for 35-40 minutes. Let cool for 5 minutes before serving.

Beef & Noodle Casserole

Ingredients:

1 pound lean ground beef
8 ounces dry wide egg noodles, cooked according to package directions (subtract 1 minute from shortest cooking time)
1/2 cup green onions, thinly sliced
1 cup sharp cheddar cheese, shredded
1 cup cottage cheese
1 (15 ounce) can tomato sauce
1/4 teaspoon garlic powder
3/4 cup sour cream
salt and pepper to taste

Preparation:

Preheat oven to 350 degrees.

Coat a 9x13 baking dish generously with non-stick spray or grease with butter.

In a skillet, brown ground beef with garlic powder and salt & pepper. Drain. Add tomato sauce and bring to a boil. Reduce to a simmer on low for 5 minutes.

In a large bowl, combine cottage cheese, sour cream and green onions. Season with salt & pepper. Add noodles and toss to coat. Add beef mixture and stir to combine. Pour into baking dish and sprinkle with cheddar cheese.

Bake for 20-25 minutes.

Ranch Chicken & Bacon Bake

Ingredients:

8 ounces dry rotini pasta, cooked according to package directions

1 cup mozzarella cheese, shredded

1/2 cup cheddar cheese, shredded

1 tablespoon olive oil

1 tablespoon dry Ranch salad dressing mix

4 slices bacon, diced

2 boneless skinless chicken breasts, cut into 1-inch chunks

 2 tablespoons fresh parsley, chopped

Sauce Ingredients:

3 cloves garlic, minced

1/4 cup parmesan, grated

2 tablespoons unsalted butter

1 cup heavy cream

salt and pepper to taste

Preparation:

Preheat oven to 375 degrees.

Coat a 9x13 baking dish generously with non-stick spray or grease with butter.

Prepare the sauce. In a saucepan, melt butter over medium heat. Add garlic and cook for 1 minute. Slowly whisk in heavy cream, continually whisking for 1-2 minutes or until smooth. Add parmesan and cook until melted. Season with salt & pepper and set aside.

In a skillet, cook bacon over medium high heat until brown, about 7 minutes. Remove bacon to a plate lined with paper towels. When bacon is cooled, chop into pieces. Reserve bacon fat in skillet.

Add 1 tablespoon of olive oil, ranch dressing mix and chicken to a Ziploc bag. Shake bag to coat.

Heat bacon fat in skillet and add chicken. Cook about 2-3 minutes on each side and set aside.

Spread pasta evenly in baking dish. Add a layer of chicken and then alfredo sauce. Top with mozzarella and cheddar. Sprinkle bacon on top.

Bake for 20 minutes and garnish with parsley.

SIDES

Mexican Rice & Beans Casserole

Ingredients:

6 cups cooked brown rice
3 cups Mexican blend cheese, shredded
2 tablespoons tomato paste
½ cup refried beans
1 (10-ounce) can Rotel diced tomatoes with chilies
2 tablespoons Mexican seasoning (recipe below)
Garnish: chopped cilantro

Mexican Seasoning Ingredients:

1 1/2 teaspoons onion powder
1 1/2 teaspoons paprika
1 tablespoon cumin
1 tablespoon chili powder
1 1/2 teaspoons garlic powder
Yields: 3 ½ tablespoons

Preparation:

Preheat oven to 375 degrees.

Coat a 9x13 baking dish generously with non-stick spray or grease with butter.

In a large bowl, add brown rice, tomato paste, tomatoes,

refried beans, 2 cups of cheese and Mexican seasoning. Mix well. Salt & pepper to taste. Spread mixture evenly into baking dish. Top with remaining shredded cheese.

Bake for 15 minutes and garnish with cilantro.

Twice Baked Potato Casserole

Ingredients:

7 medium red potatoes, baked and cut into 1-inch cubes
2 cups sharp cheddar cheese, shredded
2 cups mozzarella cheese, shredded
salt and pepper to taste
1 pound bacon, cooked and chopped
3 cups sour cream
3 green onions, sliced

Preparation:

Preheat oven to 350 degrees.

Coat a 9x13 baking dish generously with non-stick spray or grease with butter.

Place half of potatoes in baking dish. Season with salt & pepper and add half of the bacon. Spread half of the sour cream and add half of each cheese on top. Repeat layers with potatoes, salt & pepper, rest of bacon, sour cream and cheeses.

Bake for 20-25 minutes and garnish with green onions.

Cheesy Green Bean Casserole

Ingredients:

6 cups (1.5 pounds) fresh green beans, trimmed and cut into 1-inch pieces

2 cups extra sharp cheddar cheese, shredded and divided

4 1/2 teaspoons extra-virgin olive oil, divided

1/4 teaspoon onion powder

3 shallots, minced

1 cup milk

3 tablespoons dry breadcrumbs

1/3 cup all-purpose flour

2 teaspoons fresh thyme, chopped

1/4 cup dry sherry

8 ounces mushrooms, finely chopped

1 tablespoon unsalted butter

1 cup low-sodium chicken broth

1/2 teaspoon paprika

1/2 teaspoon salt

1/4 teaspoon pepper

Preparation:

Preheat oven to 425 degrees.

Coat a 9x13 baking dish generously with non-stick spray or grease with butter.

Steam green beans until crisp-tender. Run under cold water to prevent further cooking and drain well.

In a skillet, heat butter and oil over medium high heat. Add shallots and cook for about 3 minutes, or until golden. Stir in mushrooms, salt & pepper and thyme. Cook for 4 minutes.

Pour in sherry and cook for 3 minutes, stirring occasionally. Add flour and stir until all flour is wet. Pour in milk and broth. Bring to a boil and reduce to a simmer for about 5 minutes. Remove from heat.

Add 1½ cups of cheese to skillet with mushroom mixture. Add green beans and stir to coat. Pour into baking dish and top with remaining cheese.

In a small bowl, mix breadcrumbs and ½ teaspoon oil together. Stir in paprika and onion powder. Crumble over ingredients in baking dish.

Bake for 20-25 minutes. Let rest for 15 minutes before serving.

Squash Casserole

Ingredients:

1 1/2 pounds squash, sliced
1 teaspoon salt
30 Ritz crackers, crushed
1/2 sweet onion, chopped
2 tablespoons butter
1/4 cup butter, melted
1 can cream of mushroom soup
1/2 green bell pepper, chopped
4 teaspoons dry chicken bouillon
1 1/2 cups cheddar cheese, shredded
2 eggs
1/2 teaspoon black pepper

Preparation:

Preheat oven to 325 degrees.

Coat a 9x13 baking dish generously with non-stick spray or grease with butter.

Melt butter in a skillet over medium heat. Add onion, squash and bell pepper. Cook until soft and return from heat.

In a large bowl, combine ¼ cup of melted butter, soup, eggs, chicken base and cheese. Mix well. Add in vegetables and stir to combine. Pour into baking dish. Sprinkle with crushed crackers.

Bake for 20 minutes.

Cheesy Broccoli Casserole

Ingredients:

20 Ritz crackers, crushed
1 1/2 cups extra sharp cheddar cheese, shredded
4 cups broccoli, chopped
1/2 stick of butter, melted
1/4 teaspoon pepper
1 can of cream of chicken soup
2 large eggs, slightly beaten
1 cup mayonnaise
1/2 teaspoon salt
1/2 medium yellow onion, finely chopped

Preparation:

Preheat oven to 350 degrees.

Coat a 9x13 baking dish generously with non-stick spray or grease with butter.

Steam broccoli until fork-tender, being careful not to overcook. Chop broccoli into pieces and place in a medium bowl. Pour in butter, onion, mayonnaise, soup, eggs and salt & pepper. Stir to combine. Mix in ¾ cup of cheese. Spread mixture into baking dish and top with remaining cheese. Sprinkle with crushed crackers.

Bake for 30 minutes or until golden brown.

Loaded Scalloped Potato Bake

Ingredients:

8 cup Yukon Gold potatoes, thinly sliced

2 1/2 cups cheddar cheese, shredded

6 tablespoons butter

1 cup sour cream

6 tablespoons all-purpose flour

1/3 cup chives, chopped

3 cups half and half

1/2 teaspoon pepper

2 cups bacon, cooked and chopped

1 teaspoon salt

1 1/2 teaspoons garlic powder

Preparation:

Preheat oven to 350 degrees.

Coat a 9x13 baking dish generously with non-stick spray or grease with butter.

Thinly slice potatoes and boil in a stock pot with salted water for about 10 minutes, or until tender. Drain well and set aside.

In a saucepan, melt butter over medium heat. Whisk in flour and cook for 1 minute. Whisk in half & half, garlic powder and salt & pepper. Bring to a boil and remove from heat. Whisk in sour cream and then stir in ½ cup of cheese.

Spread 1/3 of the potatoes in baking dish. Pour 1/3 of the sauce on top. Top with 1/3 of remaining cheese, 1/3 of the bacon and 1/3 of the chives. Repeat these steps 2 times. Cover with foil.

Bake for 45-50 minutes. Remove foil and bake an additional 5 minutes.

Cheesy Corn Casserole

Ingredients:

1 box Jiffy cornbread mix
1 (14.75 ounce) can cream corn
1 (14.75 ounce) can regular corn, drained
3/4 cup cheddar cheese, shredded
2 eggs, beaten
3/4 cup vegetable oil

Preparation:

Preheat oven to 350 degrees.

Coat a 9x13 baking dish generously with non-stick spray or grease with butter.

In a bowl, combine all ingredients. Pour into baking dish.

Bake for 55-60 minutes.

Bacon & Corn Casserole

Ingredients:

2 (12 ounce) bags frozen corn, thawed (or 4 1/2 cups fresh)
4 pieces (1/2 cup) bacon, cooked and crumbled
2 cups cheddar cheese, shredded
2 tablespoons butter, melted
2 eggs
1/4 teaspoon cayenne pepper
1/4 cup all-purpose flour
2 tablespoons chives, chopped
2 tablespoons sugar

Preparation:

Preheat oven to 325 degrees.

Coat a 9x13 baking dish generously with non-stick spray or grease with butter.

In a food processor or blender, add eggs, butter, sugar, 2 cups of corn and cayenne pepper. Pulse 3-4 times to combine.

Place corn mixture in a bowl and then add ¾ of the cheese, bacon, remaining corn and chives. Mix well. Pour into baking dish and top with remaining cheese.

Bake for 30-35 minutes or until golden brown.

Hash Brown Casserole

Ingredients:

32 ounces frozen hash browns, thawed
2 cups Colby cheese, grated
1/2 cup butter, melted
1/4 teaspoon pepper
2 cups sour cream
1 can of cream of chicken soup
1/2 cup yellow onion, finely chopped

Preparation:

Preheat oven to 350 degrees.

Coat a 9x13 baking dish generously with non-stick spray or grease with butter.

In a bowl, mix together all ingredients (except ½ cup of cheese). Pour into baking dish and sprinkle with reserved cheese.

Bake for 50-55 minutes or until golden brown.

Made in the USA
San Bernardino, CA
28 January 2018